A HUNTER'S
FIRESIDE
BOOK

A HUNTER'S FIRESIDE BOOK

Tales of Dogs, Ducks, Birds and Guns

GENE HILL

Drawings by Milton C. Weiler

WINCHESTER PRESS

For my wife, Marcia,
and my daughters Patricia and Jennifer,
who have the grace to tolerate my peculiarities
not only with understanding amusement,
but marvelously enough,
with affection.

FOREWORD

This book is a collection of monthly columns written for *Guns & Ammo* magazine. It was the Publisher, Tom Siatos, the Editor, George Martin—and of course, Bob Petersen, who gave me not only the platform but their kind encouragement, indulgence and friendship. I owe them, and the late Roy Coykendall who introduced us, my deepest gratitude.

I would not be what I am, whatever that is, without the forebearance of my mother and father, who understand my love for the out-of-doors and not only tolerated it but encouraged it for what must have seemed to them an eternity while waiting for me to "grow up."

CONTENTS

The Elephant and the Owl 1

A Boy I Envy 3

The Woodcock Gun 5

Another New Gun 8

Midnight Owls 11

$6,537.50 13

Smell Happy 15

Genius and 100 Straight 17

A South Seas Bird 19

The Old Duck Hunter 21

To Your Health 23

Good News/Bad News 24

Collecting Guns 26

Feeling Guilty 29

Save Your Marriage 31

Planting Trees 33

Shame 35

Bargains 37

The Perfect Woman 39

The Stranger	40
November	43
A Helping Hand	45
Rain	47
A Window on the Pond	50
A Mole and a Mouse	53
Telling Lies	55
"Trouble"	56
Old Tom	57
Training Children	59
Hogging Up	61
Fate	63
A Fishing Nut	65
A Christmas Story	66
How To Win	70
Culture	72
Log Fires	75
Keeping Warm	77
The Woodcock Letter	80
The 3-Bird Accident	84
Evening Songs	85
Dentists	87
Wish Books	89
Puppies? Yes!	91
The First Gun	93
Why	95
The Wood Duck Invasion	98
Optimism	100
Brush Piles	102
Friends?	105
The High Sierras	107
Be Prepared	109
Hexes and Charms	111

Memories of Misses Past 113
Bad Cooks 115
The Elephant Hunt 117
Good Words 120
Free Advice 121
The Primrose Path 123
Witnesses 126
Going Back 128
Why Not? 130
An Evening Walk 132
The Wager 134
Raising Puppies, I 136
Jennifer Asks "Why?" 138
The Perfect Gun 140
Getting Ready 142
Sweet Dreams 145
Raising Puppies, II 146
The Old Songs 148
Hunter's Moon 151
September 153
A Christmas Wish 155
Flinching 156
Daydreams 158
The Funeral 160

THE ELEPHANT
AND THE OWL

Allow me to introduce myself. I always think it's nice to know something about the guy who claims to be an outdoor writer, as much as I always dread someone recognizing my name at a shoot or in a hunting lodge; his gun is broken and he's sure I can fix it. Let me assure you right now, once and for all, that I don't really know a trigger sear from Adam's off ox. If you ever meet me, tell me a funny story; or brag about your dog. And before you turn away, don't feel embarrassed. I work in an office more hours than I like and I'm pale, drawn, and wouldn't demand too much on a lot full of used writers. Or even readers for that matter.

But not to be too big a disappointment to you, let me immodestly point out the other side. I like, and know something about bird dogs, retrievers, and how to hit something with a shotgun on the odd day. I probably have a lot in common with you. I neglect my work to go shooting. I lie about the quality of my dogs. I spend more money on guns and all that goes with them than I can afford. I already own too many guns and want more. I have too many dogs, and I want a Brittany Spaniel. I have too many hunting coats, and none of them is *exactly* right. I can always use a spare pair of boots. I always should have been there yesterday or last week or next week; but I never will be—the die is cast. My shooting buddies always get more easy shots than I do;

and better guides. I get lost, wet, cold and tired first. If I steal an apple it's wormy. I'm on the wrong deer stand and in the quail cover that's so thick with honeysuckle that I couldn't shoot if there were birds there—but they aren't anyway. I'm either in the old man's squad at skeet or trap, the ladies' squad, or the one when the wind blows like hell. But I love clay targets, deserted deer stands, swamps, cold duck blinds, and briar patches full of quail.

I'll probably see you somewhere along the line in the kind of place we see too little of. A small lodge room with a hot pine fire and a wet dog to give a little character to the smoke. We'll sit and chat and swear we could shoot each other's gun a damn sight better than our own. We'll trade a little bourbon whiskey back and forth and talk about imaginary dogs named after ones we've got. We'll ask each other "How'd you do?" And one of us will have had too many shirts on to shoot well and the other too few to be warm enough to score. My gun is either too old or too new; I'm not used to it or it doesn't fit me any more. I'll guarantee I've got the wrong sized shot. But the nicest thing about all this—and why we're really there is not the birds brought down at all—is just to be away. "To see the elephant and hear the owl" is all there is. Give me one old gander honking for his mate, a V of green wings black against the evening sun, a cold north wind that spits a little snow across my brow, and I'll be back tomorrow, given half a chance. That's why you and I will get along so well; you'll be out there too. Offer me some of your cold coffee and half a sandwich. I've probably left mine back in the car.

A BOY I ENVY

I RECENTLY was fortunate enough to be able to order my first truly custom-made shotgun. (I won't name the make, since a lot of people have mixed emotions about my shooting ability and it might act as a depressant to this particular manufacturer's sales.) But let me tell you it's a thrill to fill up a couple of pages of paper with detail on engraving, checkering, and choke boring. Trigger pulls, shape of rib, and the finish on the wood—all as prescribed to be as much of me as the color of my hair. Now when I was all through with this I lit up my pipe and started wandering a bit back in time to a boy I remember very well. A boy who cut and carried wood for the kitchen stove. A boy who read his outdoor adventure books by the light of a kerosene lamp—whose wildest dreams could stretch to British Columbia and the land of the silver fox. And a boy whose more practical life centered around the unimaginable difficulty of saving enough money to buy five shotgun shells—in a time when a whole box of 25 sold for 65 cents. Or a summer of chores dedicated to the purchase of a dozen Blake & Lamb traps. My over-the-knee boots sold at the general store in Stillwater for a dollar a pair. My first shotgun was a six-dollar single-shot 20 gauge.

But, a boy with a trapline never thinks he's poor. There's always a tomorrow . . . there's always the next set . . . there's

3

always the possibility of the lucky catch of a fox or the skillful success of a mink set coming true. I considered myself lucky indeed to live by a good bass lake. In the first place, I worked as a fishing guide—which meant rowing the boat for a sport from pre-dawn to dark for 25 cents a day. And in the second place I got to know every inch of the shoreline worth trapping.

As it generally does for all of us, things worked out fine. I got a pretty good schooling in what they used to call "hardwood college." I always had my own dog. And often a more-or-less pet possum or coon.

Well, I sealed the envelope that held my special order details and a check that would have supported my whole family back in the old days for almost a year. I really want this new gun and I've worked long and hard for it. But if you really wanted me to look you right square in the eye and be honest, I still envy a boy I know very well, and remember—with a sense of loss—the incredible excitement of his having one dollar in his corduroy knickers on his walk to the store to buy a new pair of over-the-knee rubber boots.

THE WOODCOCK GUN

THINK FOR a minute about someone, anyone, you'd like to sit down with in front of a good log fire and talk about bird hunting. Between you sits a bottle of Virginia Gentleman bourbon, Angostura bitters and an ice bucket with dogs on it. The glasses are huge, sweating and have the smell and color of October.

My man is a good friend I've never met. Yet I'm sure that where he lives right now is just a fine, freshening walk from some alder bottoms where the woodcock fly like bats at sundown—and the surrounding gentle hills are salt-and-peppered with birches and spruce trees and therein live the Lord's own pet flock of grouse.

I'd like to meet him there someday because I own his gun. Let's say I have it in safe keeping for the time being and will someday pass it on to someone else—some other woodcock nut.

It's a little English Greener, 16 gauge, 24-inch barrels side-by-side, bored half choke and improved. It has a top safety (a rarity in a Greener) and a superb selective single trigger, with just a whisper of a pistol grip and a leather covered recoil pad. The stock is, of course, Circassian. The receiver is in the grey and gently scrolled. It's just shy of 5¾ pounds—but you wouldn't think it weighed that much; it's just there, and it flies to the shoulder like a shadow. It was made in Birmingham, England, back in 1912. It cost 56 pounds, about $280, back in those old hard money days. According to the letter I got from Greener, it was sold, special order, to this friend of mine, through the long forgotten Boston Hardware Company. They never knew his name or where he really lived. How I'd like to know the man that had it made! He must have been an independent Yankee cuss. I'll bet it was the only 24-inch side-by-side in all New England. There must have been some laughs and jokes around the cider mill when he first showed it off!

I like to think I know just how he dressed. An old felt hat with the crown pushed down all around so it would make a watering cup for his dog. And for comfort's sake he'd have had his wife cut the long sleeves off his once brown hunting coat. (Wind and rain must have bleached the canvas to butternut.) I suspect he wore a necktie when he shot his birds.

In the back of his hunting buggy, drawn by some sweet-breathed old mare, would be just-turned apple cider and some bitter ale, wrapped in dampened feed sacks to keep them cool and, without a doubt, some corn meal cakes for his old Gordon setter.

He would be getting on in years when he had the little Greener 16 made. I suspect the time had come to save those steep New England apple orchard hillside covers for some other day that rarely came. But you know how hard it is to pass by those crisp Fall Pippins, Northern Spies, or huge Pound Sweets. (My greying Labrador likes nothing better than to sit and chew stolen apples while I smoke my pipe—I think he would have liked old Tippy.)

My best guess is that this little Greener was born for the alder bottoms and the mythical flights of woodcock; if you like woodcock, you love the swamps. I'm sure he had one absolutely perfect bottom cover. There'll be one or two small creeks that pass near by. Not too much heavy grass because the farmer turns his dry cows out here to graze and fertilize the ground and feed the earthworms that the woodcock banquet on. And deep inside these alders is one perfect, cold clear spring. This whole cover's not too big— I'd guess a damned good 30-minute hunt at most. It must be wet, but not too wet. Warm, but not hot. Changing air, but not windy. And being just exactly right, it hunts best by walking East since we're sure he saves it, being best, for last, and wouldn't want the setting sun shining in his eyes.

His old Gordon setter, saddled black and tan, must have really loved this bottom. A nice cool drink, soft mud on his tired feet and best of all, the lovely umber-colored smell of woodcock. Three more birds in the bag with five handloaded shells—and back to the buggy. Cider or ale, rat cheese, hard bread, fill the pipe, cluck the mare awake and down the old dirt road. The old setter listens to the creaking axle springs, snuggles in the fresh marsh hay under the seat for a little nap and home just after dark.

My Labrador, grey-chinned Tippy, looks up at me as I put the little Greener back under the hand-rail on the crooked stairs that wind behind my fireplace. How often has this gun been wiped with loving care, swung one last time, and set away in some home-made deerhorn rack to be admired?

Here's a toast to you, old friend, who made this perfect gun come true. All Good. And I promise that as long as woodcock whistle and good dogs sleep at our feet while we sit before the fire and drink whiskey . . . you'll be remembered.

ANOTHER NEW GUN

I WAS just sort of talking out loud the other night, to myself and Tip, the old Labrador who understands such things, about how much I'd like to own a new gun. "*What* new gun?" my wife threw in from over some mending. "I thought you owned at least one of everything . . . no, I don't mean that . . . I mean one of everything and *two sets of barrels!*" So I patiently went through the fact that seeing as how we live in an advanced, international era of technology there were several sorts of new guns around from countries not as yet represented in my gun closet . . . a fact that I didn't feel was fair since they're the ones that need the most encouragement. She started reciting from memory that, for a fact, I owned guns from Australia, Germany, England . . . and for all she knew about what I had hidden away in the barn there might be stuff from Albania, Outer Mongolia, or the Baffin Islands . . . and so on.

It was quite a while before I restored any kind of calm . . . you know how some women are when they get the bit in their teeth over hardware you can't use to clean rugs with or cut grass. But I wanted to enlighten her so she wouldn't embarrass me in front of my shooting buddies so I hung in there until she paused for breath somewhere between Tierra del Fuego and Micronesia. I

8

went on, patiently, that there were a couple of guns around now that came from Italy. The land of Michelangelo and the Caesars had finally gotten around to exporting something a fellow could come to grips with besides movie stars. "How much does it cost?" she asked me. I said that I hadn't even said what it *was*. She said that it obviously was some kind of super trap gun and she didn't care *what* it was, but she did care about *how much* it was. I said that it was a new Perazzi, that Ithaca imported to help out the balance of trade relations between the United States and Italy . . . and that Ithaca probably lost money on it, et cetera, et cetera, since it was more of a good will gesture than anything else, et cetera.

She had, by now, quit the mending and was paying more than polite attention. She asked "how much?" a couple of more times and finally I said that I thought the Perazzi that I kind of leaned toward, the MX 8 model, could be picked up for around $1500. She let that sit on her mind a minute or so and then kind of leaned back and smiled and commenced to get back to the sewing. I figured that was the logical end of the discussion and went back to rubbing Tippy under her chin to make her smile. I had my fingers under Tip's collar and she was beaming away when the voice of my conscience put the mending down again and said, "Only $1500? I don't see why not because, obviously, you really need it. We can probably get about $200 by selling the rugs . . . another $500 for the furniture—that's $700. My two old winter coats are worth about $10 apiece and if we cut out the riding lessons for the kids, sell my grandmother's silver service and . . ." Well, she went on until she had stripped the house, impoverished the kids, and was reduced to wearing feed bags while she went to welfare for food coupons . . . but she finally got up the mental $1500.

I waited until she had finished and said to the dog, "See that, Tip. You aren't the only smart female in this house that knows you can't shoot trap with any living room rug!"

"Yes," she continued, "if we really did have an extra $2000 we didn't know what to do with, I wouldn't mind seeing you have your fourth or fifth really fine, first-class gun." I reminded her that it only cost $1500 for a Perazzi. "And with the other $500 left over

I'd like to have a really fine, first-class winter coat." I was about to ask what in the world she needed another winter coat for when I felt old Tip reach up and tug my hand. I understood what she meant and shut up.

MIDNIGHT OWLS

A COUPLE of years ago Ed Zern and I were sitting around in front of the fire with our feet up on the Labradors discussing one of our favorite topics—the humanitarian benefits and salubrious effects of sniffing wood smoke while drinking Virginia Gentleman, Jack Daniel's, or Wild Turkey bourbon.

The fire was getting a little sparse, so I filled my pipe with a fresh handful of Edgeworth to avoid contaminating my lungs with fresh night air, and we sauntered outside for a trip to the woodpile. Then, from the moonlit stand of shagbark hickory across the brook, we heard the calling of owls. Not just two or three owls, but owls in number.

If there was ever wild music made to go with a mid-November moonlight, cold and brittle, it is the mysterious, unseen, fluting of the owls. The presence of owls to the hunter is a humbling thing late on a November night. The murmuring of owls is more an accent to the dark silence than a wild cry.

Who can stand surrounded by this invisible, silent, disembodied sound and not be taken to the core of his very existence with the feeling of perpetual midnight. For the coming of the owls, to many, is the coming of the end. Silent in flight . . . death riding behind the scimitar beak and talons stretched out like small but absolutely inescapable rakes to earthbound living things.

When the owls cry and the dark world is swept by these mottled wings all beneath must shudder in their beds.

Logs in hand, Ed and I came back to the hearth. Smaller, wiser and completely quiet. What could we say now that had more depth than what we had just been privileged to hear. Few things could penetrate to the meaning of life and death and the world of the wild as can the overriding summoning of the owls. One last drink. Then off to restless sleep still with the sound of the owls from the shagbark hickories across the brook, throwing a different kind of blanket over the night, over the world, over our very lives.

$6,537.50

THERE ARE in life a lot of phrases that sound magnificent and truthful but in fact carry the real burden concealed—much like the iceberg. Among the more familiar are marriage vows, New Year's resolutions, fishing stories, poker winnings, and estimates of how much it will cost to go shooting. Put another way it's "There are lies and *damn* lies."

If you are among the many that have not so far ventured to embrace either trap or skeet, let me give you a glimpse as to what lies under the surface—like the murderous part of the iceberg.

You ask your buddy who sports "25 STRAIGHT" patches over his imported, custom-made, silk shooting jacket, "How much does it cost to shoot skeet?" He, in truth, says (especially if his wife is in earshot; remember, wives are *always* in earshot), "Oh, clay targets run to about a nickel apiece . . . a dollar twenty-five a round. Plus shells, of course . . . brings it to about three-and-a half bucks."

You, a sweet, white-robed innocent, figure three or four times three-and-a-half bucks—not an unlikely sport. It can be swung. And indeed it could, if what your buddy said was even up to being a half-truth.

Here is a short summary of what you must add to the $3.50 it costs to shoot a round of trap or skeet. Shooting jacket, shooting glasses, shooting gloves, shooting hat. (You think you have these or can make do? Wrong. You will feel like the first gal at the beach to show up in a topless bathing suit.) There are in fact, shooting shirts, shooting ties, shooting pants, shooting belts, shooting shoes and socks. But these come later. You *must* play poker, gin rummy, or pinochle between rounds. You will probably lose. Your turn to buy a round will come when everyone has just switched from beer to Jack Daniel's. They might be doubles. You will be badgered into membership in the NSSA, ATA, NRA, PITA, one or more wild-life organizations, and tickets to the next police function.

As I said, this is only a superficial summary. The details vary and are really not important; they depend somewhat on local custom. What you should know is that the grand total to shoot a round of skeet or trap will amount to roughly $6,537.50. But don't be disheartened. Look at the positive side: don't think of it as expensive, think of all the things that cost more: an African safari, a Rolls-Royce, a matched pair of Purdeys . . . or a Mexican divorce.

SMELL HAPPY

I WISH I knew more about the phenomenon of scent. I remember a night, years and years past, when I had old Red, our coon hound, in the front seat of the Model A when a big coon scurried across the road in front of us. I shoved Red out and brought him over to where I had just seen the coon cross. Red looked up at me as if I was crazy and climbed back into the car. We came down the same road about a half hour later and I had another crack at it and this time Red took off, bawling furiously on the track. Why not when it was immediately fresh? How do dogs know which direction to go in?

Do they have a vocabulary of scents? Do they know a coon from a possum? Do they just "like" some smells better than others?

One of my English setters wouldn't dream of pointing a rabbit, but I'll bet she's pointed a million or more field mice. I never had the chance to find out but I've always wondered if a bird dog would point a wild duck. (It's often been suggested that it's a miracle any of my dogs ever smelled anything, since most of my waking hours are involved with my pipe and the air in the station wagon can get pretty heavy.)

I'd give anything to know what a woodcock or quail smells like to a pointing dog but that goes in with the rest of the things I'll be denied.

That pipe is one of the reasons I guess I can't smell anything much myself, but I know some shooters who've crawled around the ground and tried sniffing out pheasants and quail. Some say they can, but I remain a long way this side of being convinced.

But I can sniff out a thunderstorm coming and if you ever want somebody to join you in great nosefuls of early summer, I'm your boy! I like the green smell of the budding swamps, the silver smell of a freshening brook as much as I like the orange and yellow smells of falling leaves and drying hay.

I also imagine (which is just as good as being sure) that I can smell the difference between a North wind and a West wind; even the extremes of the full moon and the dark.

They say animals can smell fear in an enemy—or in a man, and I believe that. But on the more positive side I also believe that animals, ourselves included, can smell joy, good humor, honesty, and decency.

If in a single day we smell coffee, dawn, gun oil, powder, a wet dog, woodsmoke, bourbon, and the promise of a West wind for a fair tomorrow—and it's possible for us to reek "happy"— that's just what we will do.

GENIUS AND 100 STRAIGHT

I DON'T know what most of you expect from me in the way of improving your lot in life and you'll have to grant that I have never hinted that I was a genius. Brilliant, now and then, but genius—never! But you never know where lightning or brains will strike next.

I was in the midst of a fascinating chat with Derek Partridge about choke boring and patterns and we got to wondering why two such magnificent shots as we admitted easily to be, ever missed a trap target. After all, the shots are more similar than different in any given round and if you can break five in a row there is no good solid reason why a man with some given talent shouldn't go on to break 100.

Derek allowed as how if he lifted his head he'd probably miss a clay and I agreed that that was the one unforgiving fault in a man who is generally considered a sensational shot. Then suddenly it struck me! I felt like Archimedes who began shouting Eureka when the solution to the displacement of water by an immersed body struck him. "Eureka!" I shouted. Partridge looked a trifle questioning about my mental stability and got up to refill my glass. I hastily motioned him to sit back down and be quiet. "Derek, old chum," I said, "You are in the presence of genius. Pure, 24-carat gold genius. I have just this instant solved the problem of a shooter ever lifting his head in competition." Partridge made another move to refill my bourbon and again I hastily motioned him back.

I needed a few minutes of absolute quiet to revel in the glow of such incredible inspiration. "Derek, do you know what Velcro is?" I asked him. But without giving him time to answer I went on. "Velcro is a fabric closure. Like a zipper. It was invented by a man who spent a lot of his time looking at the spines on cockleburrs—probably trying to pick them out of a bird dog. Anyway, Velcro is fabric woven, or something, to resemble the little hooks on a burr. You press the two pieces of cloth together and they stay together until you gently pull them apart. Understand?" Derek nodded his head. The look on his face reflected that he was mulling over the coincidence between genius and insanity.

"Derek . . . listen . . . and listen hard. What if you have a Velcro band-aid thing on your cheek. And a patch of Velcro on your gun stock. How in hell are you going to lift up your head??? You can't without really tugging . . . a quick lift would free the gun enough to take it down to reload—but I guarantee you won't pick your face off the stock enough to miss targets!!"

Apparently the idea was too huge a concept for him to grasp immediately so he mumbled something about an early morning flight and left.

I remained nearly sleepless the whole night. How could I patent the idea . . . should the Velcro be flesh colored . . . can Velcro be stained to match Circassian walnut . . . would the Amateur Trapshooting Association outlaw it . . . my mind raced like a puppy until the obvious answer came to mind. I would give my idea to all. Trapshooters from every corner of the globe would speak my name in hushed tones.

And now the deed is done. I have the deep pleasure to bestow my revelation on each and every one of you. And you may rest assured that my every conscious moment is now devoted to handling those tricky angles on stations one and five. The solution to those, you can be well assured, is near at hand.

You're welcome.

Lewis & Clark
slept here
(146 times)

FORT MANDAN AND THE
NORTH DAKOTA LEWIS & CLARK
INTERPRETIVE CENTER

WASHBURN, ND
www.fortmandan.com

Fort Mandan

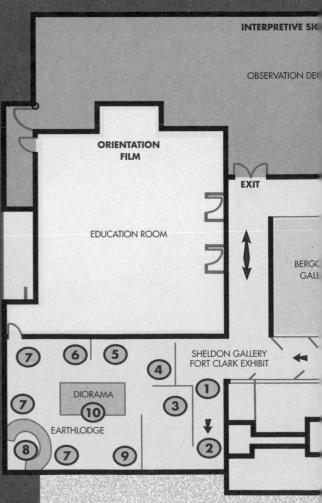

The Corps of Discovery constructed Fort Mandan to serve as a winter home during their stay here in 1804-1805. Construction began on November 2, and the Expedition celebrated its completion on December 25, 1804.

Built entirely of cottonwood trees from the shores of the Missouri River, seven rooms housed the men, two stored supplies and food, and one served as the blacksmith's shop. Eight fireplaces were built back to back between the rooms. The outside walls of the fort stretched eighteen feet high, with roofs sloping inward to about seven feet.

Above each room, a loft provided a sleeping area for many of the soldiers. A walkway above the storehouses made it possible for guards to protect the back and sides of the Fort.

Two large doors opened toward the river during the day, and were usually locked at sunset each night. The interior walls were chinked with a mixture of river clay and grass to keep the warmth from the fireplaces within the rooms.

This full-sized, furnished replica of Fort Mandan was built by the McLean County Historical Society in 1972. It is now managed by the Lewis & Clark Fort Mandan Foundation, a private non-profit organization.

INTERPRETIVE SIG

OBSERVATION DE

ORIENTATION FILM

EXIT

EDUCATION ROOM

BERG
GALL

7 6 5

4

DIORAMA 10

3

SHELDON GALLERY
FORT CLARK EXHIBIT

1

7

EARTHLODGE

8 7 9

2

The Must Sees...

The North Dakota Lewis & Clark Interpretive Center has something for everyone!

Harmony Park - Giant metal sculptures of Lewis, Clark and Chief Sheheke welcome you.

History Buffs - Engaging displays of rare artifacts are found throughout the Center.

Art Lovers - The Bergquist Gallery houses a complete collection of Karl Bodmer's historic artwork.

Travelers - The Fort Clark Exhibit recounts the stories of the many who followed Lewis & Clark.

Kids (and the kid in all of us) - Interactive wonders that challenge, entertain and put the past at your fingertips.

Fort Mandan's open gates invite you to step inside and back in time!

Just down the hill, 2 1/2 miles west on County Road 17, Fort Mandan looks as if the expedition never left! The fully furnished rooms provide the sights, sounds and smells of the Corps of Discovery's winter at Fort Mandan.

On the Fort Mandan History and Nature Trail, winding through the cottonwoods along the Missouri River, you'll learn of the many early inhabitants of the area. It's a short, 20 minute walk with lots of picture stops.

The North Dakota Lewis & Clark Interpretive Center is at Washburn, ND, 38 miles north of Bismarck at the junction of Highways 83 and 200A. Fort Mandan is 2 1/2 miles west of the Interpretive Center on County Road 17. Our facilities are open all year. Memorial Day through Labor Day, 9 a.m. to 7 p.m; remainder of the year 9 a.m. to 5 p.m.

For more information on special events, current exhibits or group tours, you may write us at Lewis & Clark Fort Mandan Foundation, P.O. Box 607, Washburn, ND 58577, call us at (877) 462-8535 or visit our website, www.fortmandan.com.

Admission
Adults $7.50 • Students $5.00 • Members Free!

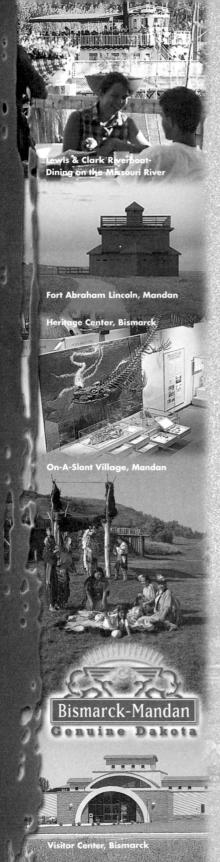

Lewis & Clark Riverboat-Dining on the Missouri River

Fort Abraham Lincoln, Mandan

Heritage Center, Bismarck

On-A-Slant Village, Mandan

Bismarck-Mandan
Genuine Dakota

Visitor Center, Bismarck

The Whole Package

Tours

We offer a selection of tours for groups visiting our sites with special discounts if reservations are made in advance. This service is offered year round. Along with tours, special educational programs are available by request.

Room Rentals

Room rentals are available at the North Dakota Lewis and Clark Interpretive Center. Rooms can be arranged as needed for your gathering. Electronic equipment is available in these rooms with seating for up to 170 people.

Picnic Shelters

Three large picnic shelters are available at the Fort Mandan site with a 150-person capacity each. Reservations are accepted for the picnic shelters for a nominal fee.

Other Services

- Join our volunteer programs. Please ask for information.
- We have special events sponsored by the Foundation. Please ask for a calendar of events.
- Ask about the Traveling Exhibits and Special Interpretive Programs we offer.

Member Benefits

Members of the Lewis & Clark Fort Mandan Foundation are admitted free to the Interpretive Center and Fort Mandan, and receive valuable discounts in our gift shops. Ask about a membership and save money today!

> **Interpretive Center and Fort Mandan**
> **Reservations - (877) 462-8535**

Just Down the River

Lewis and Clark found a warm welcome here, and you will too, both in Washburn and in Bismarck-Mandan.

Today the tradition is carried on through the Bismarck-Mandan Visitor Center, filled with helpful information and people to better guide you.

When you're ready to make camp, follow the trail to Bismarck-Mandan, with a choice of more than 2,300 sleeping rooms, over a hundred distinctive restaurants, and a wide variety of attractions, specialty shops and malls.

1-800-767-3555 • bismarckmandancvb.com
Exit 157 off I-94 • 1600 Burnt Boat Dr.

A SOUTH SEAS BIRD

I WAS having lunch with a friend, let's call him George, at one of those topless restaurants in California, when for some reason he suddenly remembered that he wanted to get a new recoil pad fitted on his 20-gauge side-by-side. A while later when we were in the car headed for Pachmayr Gun Works, I remarked to George that he seemed to have nothing but guns and shooting on his mind and mentioned the old "all work and no play" adage. To further the point, I told him the story about the avid birdshooter who had sort of been dragooned into serving as part of the crew (between seasons, of course) on one of those Pacific sailing races.

They hadn't been out too long when a terrific storm came up and our friend was washed overboard. When he came to, he found he was on a lovely island and an exquisite young girl was offering him a mixture of rum and coconut milk to help restore his senses. As soon as she saw him recovering she ran off into the lush jungle but quickly returned with some cold remains of what had been a succulent roasted pig. Now, all his senses restored, he began to sit up and take notice of his surroundings. He couldn't help but notice the young lady was as scantily clad as she was beautiful. Then she rolled over to him, cradled his head in her arms and whispered "Strange man . . . before someone comes to rescue you, you and

I are going to a secret place and I will make you very happy, but you must promise never to tell a soul."

Then she smiled again, the fragrance of her skin flooding his senses and said, "Do you know what I mean?"

"You bet I do," he said, "you've got woodcock shooting on this island and I'll never tell anybody!"

George thought about the story for a minute, narrowly avoiding an old lady with orange hair driving a Sting Ray, and said, "She must have been mistaken . . . there is a Pacific *snipe* that looks a little like a woodcock but . . ."

THE OLD DUCK HUNTER

THE Old Duck Hunter died the other day, 75 years old and suddenly he's gone like a black in full flight.

But the things he took with him! The stories that only he could tell—because only he remembered. The subtle inflection, the nicety of a turn of phrase, the eye lost to use for a minute while it turned backward . . . 40 . . . 50 . . . 60 years. Everything was different then in the times gone long ago. I'm sure the hay smelled sweeter in the fall, the air was crisper, the ducks wilder and the hand polished Parkers threw better patterns with what they used to call "St. Louis 3's." The clothes were tougher, the whiskey smoother, the weather sharper, and they shot bigger and smarter birds and more of them.

God! How I miss it. I could listen with closed eyes and see the fieldstone fireplaces in the legendary, long-lost duck clubs blazing with the crack of pine knots that talked back while busily sludging smoke into the spitting promise of tomorrow's squall. Not many left who knew and drank and gunned and laughed with the likes of Shang Wheeler, Joel Barber, and Colonel Sheldon.

He was an old young man, whatever that means. Just a few days ago we had drinks together. Old Forester on the rocks with a touch of bitters for him and I think I had a martini. We didn't talk for the first few minutes, just stood at the bar and steeped in the pleasure of each other's company. We liked each other and words never seemed necessary at first or even appropriate. Then we began chatting about guns and duck loads. As usual he favored 4's and I favored 6's. He liked oversized decoys and I agreed. And we ordered lunch. He was a spare man, and tough. But we kidded a lot. I teased him about his skeet shooting and he reminded me that trap shooters were often seen in the field without neckties. Lunch was over and he remarked that he wasn't feeling well and I never saw him again.

If a man can love another man I guess that I loved Ralf. I loved the things he stood for and the way he stood for them. I could tell you that I miss him but that wouldn't be saying very much. So I can't tell you anything, except that he's gone and things have changed. Duck blinds aren't exactly the same anymore and neither is bourbon whiskey. And that's a lot of change to me. A lot of change. And I'd rather not go into it more deeply, because you know what I mean. Because I can't.

I hope you have an Old Duck Hunter in your life and I hope he lives in your blind . . . and shares your whiskey forever. Like Ralf, I'm sure, will do with me. I have a hollow space that only he can fill . . . in moments that we all have between flights . . . between life's little things . . . between the distant promise in the call of geese and the sudden flare of setting wings . . . between the point and the flush . . . and in the darkening moments between the end of the day and the start of tomorrow.

TO YOUR HEALTH

RALF, WHO was often found waterfowling with a couple of us, once said that he liked to shoot geese and duck because it gave him a chance to drink whiskey for his health. One of the aforementioned "us" said that there is nothing wrong with Ralf's health and Ralf, taking an ounce of Old Forester in his coffee, said that there is nothing wrong with his ability to drink bourbon either, but "a man ought to have reason." Crosby asked what Ralf's reason was and Ralf said, topping off his Thermos cup again, "this was how he *knew* he was healthy."

Actually Ralf was drinking because last year he broke his leg and the cold weather makes it stiff. I asked him if bourbon helped loosen it up and Ralf said that "No, it didn't but if *both* legs were stiff it put him back in balance."

GOOD NEWS/BAD NEWS

Now UNLESS this fall is different than in other years, you can anticipate, if that's the word, the following things happening. You will plan a long weekend bird hunting at least 200 miles from home and after getting thoroughly lost, arrive to find that the weather is either too hot or too cold or too something and will return home to find out that your neighbor has gotten his limit of woodcock along the brook that runs behind your barn. You will be carrying two bags into the hunting lodge. One with 12-gauge shells and the other with three bottles of bourbon. One bag will break and the contents will fall on the stone steps. Which bag? And don't forget that tomorrow's Sunday and all the stores are closed.

A week before opening day of the quail season your pointer bitch will either come into a roaring heat or surprise you with a litter of illegitimate puppies. Your wife's family, whom you haven't seen for a year and a half, will suddenly arrive the same weekend duck hunting opens. It's the Sunday of your trap club's big shoot and you feel ready. Then the new neighbor who just moved in comes over and wants to go along. You say "fine." He gets his gear and you discover he owns a pair of Krieghoff trap guns and his shooting jacket is covered with "200 STRAIGHT" patches.

But we won't let these things get us down; good sports all, we come back smiling, knowing with absolute certainty that tomorrow's cover is bustling with game, the Northeast wind will chill our duck blinds on the very next go and fate will waft a cinder in the eye of the expert and you'll come through a winner after all.

The thing that cements the love of a man for his carpet of leaves and his ceiling of stars is the knowledge that just being involved is enough. There is no score worth keeping. All we should ever count is hours; never birds, nor length of horn or hits or misses. If we want to do something where we can't lose, then we must accept the proposition that we cannot win. We are not involved in a contest, but a very simple and pure journey that promises each day out will be different, unrepeatable, unrecapturable. Each time is unique. If there is anything of value to be entered in the log, let's leave it at a series of impressions. A day without birds is a day spent in delicious solitary thought, a day that might bring you closer to understanding the infinite mystery of it all.

A grown man walking in the rain with a sodden bird dog at his heel who can smile at you and say with the kind of conviction that brings the warmth out in the open "I'd rather be here, doing this, right now, than anything else in the world," is the man who has discovered that the wealth of the world is not something that is merely bought and sold.

A shaft of sunlight through a golden oak, a cock pheasant so full of life he's bragging at the world, a preening mallard hen parading a string of ducklings as if they were diamonds, the sift of snow that suddenly quiets the universe—anxious for the light to be done. This is the wealth of the world. And we are rich.

COLLECTING GUNS

ONE OF the finer points of gun collecting, if not the finest, is the ability of concealing from your wife: (1) the fact that you have actually purchased a new gun or (2) what the new gun actually cost in terms of carpeting, new fur coats, or kitchen cabinets. As a somewhat scarred veteran of this war I have been left with several suggestions that I swear have worked either for me or an accomplice.

A very simple but effective technique has proven as workable to many gun collectors as the Ruy Lopez opening in chess has proved effective to chess lovers. And it's almost as classic. Your neighbor, who doesn't shoot to your wife's certain knowledge, comes over some evening with a long parcel rather carelessly wrapped in old newspapers. *It is extremely important the newspapers be old.* The nearer the headlines are to the Battle of Jutland, the less the suspicion. (There is always suspicion . . . all we can really ever do is bring it down to where we can cope with it.) Now since you have given your neighbor, Bob, a full quart of Virginia Gentleman to play the role . . . to wear the mask . . . he has no doubt done a smidgin of rehearsal. The conversation should go something like this:

> You: Hi there, Bob! What you got all wrapped up, that old antique floor lamp you wanted me to help you re-wire?

Bob: No, and I kind of hate to bother you with this, but we run across this old gun in a second-cousin's attic the other day and he asked me if I knew anyone who'd kind of look after it for him while he's in Saudi Arabia working for the oil company.

You: I hope it's not valuable . . . if it were . . .

Bob: No, he doesn't think so. I think he got it for about ten dollars, years ago and he's been meaning to make a lamp out of it but never got around, you know.

You: Well, let's have a look. (You unwrap the gun, a magnificent single-barrel Parker trap gun that you have artfully disguised for the time being by random wrappings of old friction tape over the 24 lines-to-the-inch checkering. You casually dismiss the gun as a clunker by pushing it off to one side with your foot as you read aloud from some of the old headlines about the raiding of speakeasies or something.)

Bob: I told you it was just something he got stuck with . . . why for ten dollars . . .

You: Well, don't worry about it. I'll put a little kerosene on the rust spots so they don't get any worse and stick it out in the garage.

Bob: Well, thanks a million for your trouble. I'll tell cousin Dave that you'll hold on to it for him. Be seeing you.

You turn to your wife, and picking up the gun like it was a dead skunk you remove it quickly from sight, mentioning that she ought to take a look at the old newspapers since that seemed to be the year she was born. This will start a diverting argument that will so fully occupy the evening that the coming and going of the Parker will soon be forgotten. It is important that you never handle the gun in your wife's presence until she is so used to seeing it cluttering up the garage over in the corner where the rakes and shovels are that she'll be delighted to discover that you've put it somewhere else. Out of sight, out of mind is one of the cardinal rules of all gun acquiring.

Another useful technique is in the actual cost where it is impossible for one reason or another to conceal that you have actually bought another gun. This is known as the "New Dress Gambit," or "The Wolters Shift." Like all fine things, it is simplicity itself . . . and even if the Queen Bee *does* have the wind up and is sniffing the air like a dog on a covey, the clincher, the final sentence is guaranteed foolproof. The scene opens as you return home with a mint condition Model 12 Winchester Pigeon grade, original rib and in a heavy leather leg-o-mutton case that is alone worth at least $35. You are chuckling to yourself as if you have just done something you are beginning to think might make you feel a bit ashamed.

> WIFE: Well, what now? Don't tell me you bought another gun, when you promised me . . .
>
> YOU: (Interrupting quickly) Let me tell you what happened, see if I've done the right thing. I been saving for a while now to get a lamp for the living room that I saw at that antique shop. But I stopped in another place today and the lady asked me if I knew anybody that had any use for an old pump gun . . . and she brought out this Winchester. What'll you take for it, I asked her, not seeming to be too much interested and still wandering around the lamps. Well, she says, a lot of people are collecting old guns nowadays and I get anywhere from $35 to $50. Well, I told her that I *did* like old pump guns and I'd give her $30 for it. "Sold" she said. Well, I'd saved $50, honey, and I can sell the case for $20, so that means that I have $35 left over for you to go buy a new dress."

Here, you must *reach down and fork over the $35 in cold cash!* The transfer of cold cash and the mention of a new dress will hold her long enough for you to put the gun away, following the cardinal rule of "out of sight out of mind." While you are messing in the gun cabinet start talking about the color of the new dress. And don't worry about her changing the conversation very much. I'm sure Eve could have, and did, go on for hours about picking a new leaf from the fig tree.

FEELING GUILTY

The talk had turned in the dwindling hours of the early morning into the sort of conversation we usually reserve for the dwindling hours of the early morning. Questions like "What would you do if you had it all to do over?" kept cropping up and we fielded them rather ineptly. I think, since we were all shooting buddies, that we had more than a small sense of guilt.

The time we spent around the house doing yard chores and fooling with the kids, like most other fathers seem to do, was shamefully scant. Our houses were sparsely furnished with what seemed to be second-hand furniture. Our wives made most of their clothes or borrowed from each other. And so it went—I'm sure I don't have to tell *you*. It sort of added up to the fact that if the movies were casting for an all-American family man none of us need apply. The hours spent with the family seemed to *always* be at field trails, trap shoots, duck hunting, and chatting with daddy while he runs up half a case of trap loads.

We got to feeling pretty sorry for the small folks we were supposed to be raising and setting good examples for. It got worse for me when a much-mended chair broke for the hundredth time. Rising to get some glue I had in the gun closet, I glimpsed again the blued barrels and glistening walnut stocks of enough money to buy a good sofa and a fairly decent rug and a new stove for the kitchen.

The thing that we all were thinking, but none of us wanted to be the first to talk out loud about, was that none of our families really seemed to mind. Oh, now and then one of the wives would throw some kind of a fit, but it never seemed to be all that serious. Our women all knew how to shoot and seemed to enjoy it. So did all the kids that were big enough. One thing all the kids did know about were animals. Wild and domestic. They knew the ducks and how to handle the duck dogs. They were respectful of guns and admiring of the men who handled them exceptionally well. They enjoyed the people at shoots and field trials and vice versa. They knew how to pluck birds and some were turning into more than passable game cooks. But most important of all, none of them were less than fine human beings.

It seems to add up that men and women, no matter what their age, who take a great deal of pleasure in the out-of-doors, at the very least discover something about themselves. That they aren't the only apple in the orchard. That sportsmanship is by and large another word for good manners. And that very few things that are too easy to come by are much worthwhile. In short, we decided—not very profoundly, I'm afraid—that as a way of passing our few allotted hours, our kind of life had quite a bit to recommend it. I found a little piece from Thoreau that seemed to sum it up a bit more nicely than we had: *"I went into the woods because I wished to live deliberately, to confront only the essential facts of life, and see if I could not learn what it had to teach, and not, when I came to die, discover that I had not lived."*

SAVE YOUR MARRIAGE

UNDER THE easy guise of taking your wife's measurements for a new shotgun, you have ascertained her coat size. You then go to your local gun shop and order yourself a new gun. Since he has made a fair profit on this transaction, the dealer will be in a good mood to give you a few dollars off on something for her—a ladies' model shooting coat.

You spirit the gun away in a safe place and arrive home with a large package, neatly wrapped, which contains the jacket. She will quickly ask you "What's in the package?" (The known world's record for restraint in asking "What's in the package?" is held by Mrs. James Pierce. Time: 1 minute: 27 seconds. The reason for this incredible elapsed time is that she'd been asking her husband Jim for three weeks to stop on the way to lunch some day and get her a new ironing board cover and she assumed that he had done so. He would have, of course, but *Abercrombie & Fitch* doesn't stock ironing board covers.)

You hand her the box and prime yourself for the inevitable look of disappointment since she will immediately think it is a new shooting jacket that you have purchased for yourself and are merely letting her have the thrill of opening the box. Your next move is to slip it over her shoulders and begin Standard Shooter's Speech Number 7, which runs more or less like this: "(wife's name goes here), honey, it's about time we start doing more things to-gether. I suddenly realized that out of all the weekends last year I was only home the Sunday of the big blizzard when the car got stuck in the driveway. I don't think that's fair, do you? (Impor-tant—do not allow her time to answer because the very mention of weekends makes her angry or worse. You can assume she agrees because that fact probably occupies 90 percent of her conversa-tion—or will.) Now, Barbara Crosby goes to almost all of Dave's shoots and I want you to go along with me!!"

Now your wife is trapped. One: she has a new coat she has to wear somewhere but she cannot wear a coat full of leather shoul-der patches and shell loops to the P.T.A. tea. Two: she knows other women are there—for all she knows Barbara Crosby might be employed by the Playboy Club. Three: she can get a new pair of slacks to go with the coat.

Now you have her with you weekends at the club. She is playing cards with the other ladies. She is making you a first-class lunch so you don't have to shoot while your stomach is wrestling with the club hot dog. You have achieved, at long last, marital harmony—or, at least a reasonable facsimile thereof.

If I have enough requests I will quickly finish and publish my book, *How I Trained My Wife To Find Happiness By Reloading 500 Trap Shells An Hour In Her Spare Time*. It will, of course, be mailed to you, at the office, in a plain brown wrapper.

PLANTING TREES

In the cool of the evenings, along about now, I have taken to strolling back to the field next to the brook run. It is in this field that last spring I planted 1000 little trees, mostly white pine and fir. I just like to stand there and look at them. You get the same feeling reading a book backwards. If you like the ending, you get intrigued with the beginning. In my mind's eye I see trees 20 years or more from now. They'll be as much a part of the landscape as the setting sun. The absolutely right word for it is that they will become *permanent*. I will do something that will become permanent. In time to come I will look at these trees (here we leap forward to imagine them now 10 feet tall) and I will remember when I planted them. Straw-like, fragile wisps of plant, through my labor—and another, more important, magic which I do not understand—that have now become that special thing we call a tree.

Permanent. In more time to come there will be nothing else that brings me to the mind of people searching to remember who I was than looking at my trees. My hands dug the holes, my hands put the seedlings in the ground. My hands moved them as they grew, to the places where the sun and shadow would be best. My eyes watch them. These are my trees now—no accident of whimful nature put them in the ground where someday they will stand.

My hands do that. As long as these trees live, so will my name, I would rather have the whisper of the boughs to sing my story than a line or two etched in some cold stone. I am now my trees and they are me. That is enough to think about through this cooling evening as the light leaves—taking another day of mine with it.

SHAME

RECENTLY, AN ad ran in our local paper offering a $50 reward leading to arrest of the man who had shot a doe pregnant with twin fawns and left the remains of this butchery on the edge of the brook in a little park where the kids play after school.

Last fall, the same paper carried a notice from a man who had seen two hunters shoot his little dog just 100 yards from his house. The notice was a plea for gunners to be more careful, since this was the second little dog he had lost in the same way.

I cannot comment further on these incidents, nor do I think I have to. But I'm sure that this is not by any means an isolated example or two. The point I'd like to make is that the average sportsman doesn't give a damn about policing his own ranks. Do you insist that your hunting buddies pick up the sandwich wrappers? Or fix the fences? Or offer the farmer a bird or rabbit now and then? If you know a companion is committing an illegal act, do you have the guts to turn him in? Or if he's just plain stupid or careless, have you taken the time to give him a good talking to?

There are a lot of folks who don't use a gun but enjoy the same thrill of being outdoors amidst the game that we do. They have a couple of rights themselves. Carrying a gun or owning one doesn't grant any special privileges—what it really does is add a lot of responsibilities. Responsibilities that a lot of us are apparently unwilling to shoulder.

I don't know the details of cross-country game laws but I wouldn't object if my state had a clause that could remove a man's hunting privileges for life if he was caught shooting illegal game. Or being so carelessly stupid as to shoot a man's pet dog. As far as I'm concerned that is an illegal act. It is theft of a very base sort and might easily be ruled in the area of grand larceny and carry a similar penalty.

Until this sort of thing is stopped it should be a burden on our conscience and we should feel shame if ever we turn a blind eye to such acts among people we know.

BARGAINS

EVERY YEAR I receive a great number of letters from women who want to find a way to convince their husbands to buy another gun. Typically, this one from a Mrs. George M.:

"One of my favorite chores every week is cleaning the glass and waxing the wood on my husband's gun cases. He has the following rifles: .338, .264, 7MM, .358, .458, .243, .222, .30-30, .375, .22. Those are the numbers I can see on the barrels—so I assume they are the size of the cartridge. He has several rifles marked .30-06, and one or two different rifles with the same numbers on the barrels besides these. He won't let me shoot yet because he says I have to know all about guns first. Right now I'm learning bluing. I have all the troughs and things set up in the basement by the laundry. I've gotten quite good at it now and some of George's friends are bringing barrels over for my bluing. I'm so proud! And now George is giving me two dollars a barrel—just for bluing. I never imagined that shooting could be such fun and so profitable! He's even promised to let me try checkering and steel engraving!

"Now, here's my problem. George tells me that these rifles are expensive. Some of them cost as much as $25, he says, but for most of them he only pays about $10 or $15; of course, the long glass sight probably costs $2 or $3 extra. I have saved some money from my grocery allowance and my bluing and I know George could use another rifle. What number caliber should I get and where can I find a Mr. Weatherby, since those are the rifles he says he wants more of?"

Gentlemen, you're creating a problem. It's easy enough to get your wife to give you the $20 and say you'll contact Mr. Weatherby or Mr. Remington or Mr. Winchester yourself—but what about all these women who are less sheltered from the world than Mrs. G. M.?

I have foreseen this problem and have taken steps in our mutual behalf. I am planning to publish a monthly newsletter of gun prices and related items. All this will of course be in code—the 2's will actually mean 5's or something similar.

A column you can tear out and leave around the house is now presented for your convenience.

GUNS FOR SALE:

Winchester M21. Silver inlaid game scenes.
  28″ barrels. Mod. & Full $35.00
Parker. 20 gauge. 2 sets barrels. Skeet 26″,
  28″ IC & M. GHE grade $48.00
Weatherby .300 Magnum. Custom stock.
  4X Redfield. Inlaid sheep in gold $55.00
Krieghoff San Remo. 4 sets skeet bbls.
  12 gauge to .410. Fitted case $65.00
Ithaca 4E Trap single bbl. Orre choked.
  Fajen stock $60.00
Remington Trap loads. 12 gauge 3-7½s or 8s.
  By the case $10.00
Size-O-Matic Reloader. 1000 rounds per
  hour. Postpaid $24.95

Dummy ads can be placed in your local newspaper with a false name and address or fictitious telephone—they make a fine basis for home discussion. But don't forget to be a little more honest with the guy who's making out your will. The last time I was in the hospital, Ed Zern called up my wife and offered her $15 for my Greener double and she was damn near tempted to turn a $5 profit on it!

THE PERFECT WOMAN

I TRY TO spend a few days goose shooting in Easton, Maryland, every year with David Crosby, an old friend of mine. Crosby is one of the best wing shots and skeet shooters in our area—good enough to have the gall to occasionally show up at a registered shoot wearing linen plus-fours. In an effort to do something about the local laundry situation, Crosby married. During what turned out to be an eight-hour lull in the shooting, I asked Crosby if his bride, Barbara, was surprised when she received a shotshell reloader for Christmas, when I knew she was expecting a vacuum cleaner. Crosby said he'd be glad to buy her a new vacuum cleaner when they made one that would also turn out 200 12-gauge skeet loads an hour.

We got to discussing wives, and George Martin, who was also sleeping in the blind with us, mentioned that a friend of his had discovered the perfect woman. "And what's perfect?" I asked him.

George smiled wistfully and said, "For me, about 14½ in length of pull, 1 ⅜ at the comb and 2 inches drop at heel."

THE STRANGER

I DIDN'T think much about it. It wasn't the first time I'd shared a duck blind with someone I didn't know—by name or face. In fact, the first time I really tried to see who he was, was when he started to talk to me. There was no introduction. He never asked me my name or told me his. We were just sitting there in the pre-dawn night, two men, total strangers, sharing only the common emotions and inclinations that led us to be in the same place at the same time.

As I look back on it I think it was the remoteness of each other, the un-identity we shared, the feeling of a mutual isolation that started it all. "Do you know me or what I look like?" he said.

It struck me as a strange question, but I merely said "No."

"No matter," he answered. "I'm a middle-aged man in excellent health. Are you a doctor?" I said I wasn't. "I'm extremely fit. I do not wear glasses. Women, much younger than myself, find me an attractive male. I am quite successful in business. My wife and children are happy, healthy and charming. To the outsider—or even close neighbor—I am an envied man. I have all the outward things. And the things I have are fine. But for one." Here he stopped and I could sense he was debating whether or not to continue. I remained quiet, my curiosity so complete I was hoping that some miracle could delay dawn for at least a little while since I was convinced (and later this feeling proved to be right) that he would contrive some way to prevent me from ever knowing who he was by sight.

"The one thing that bothers me, amidst my beautiful garden," he continued, "is that no one knows me. Or even wants to." As he spoke, I paused to light a fresh pipe. "My wife doesn't know me. My children don't really know me. Needless to say the people where I work know even less. And it seems that no one really cares to know more about me. But there are things I fear and things I love. I have my dreams that are never to be. No one knows me.

"No one knows how I fear death. No one knows how much I love life. I watched a deer feed on water weeds the other day and I was so struck by the simple magnificence that I sat and cried. I cried that there was so much to do and see that I never will do and see. I live in a world where my words are only words. I cannot speak of passion. I cannot tell them what I feel about the last flight pitching in as the sun sets. Or how much I still love to put a leaf in a brook and walk beside it down the stream just to watch the way the water works. I want someone to know that here is a man who feels so deeply about his little world that he could only speak of it but once. And that he needed a total stranger for an ear. I've talked about myself before. To hunting dogs. To geese. Sometimes only to the wind.

"I am almost through my life and no one has ever asked me what I felt about the lunge of a bass, the flush of a grouse or the sudden appearance of a deer. No one will ever know, but you, how much I still miss my dogs that died. Or how hard I wish for the dream to live a special day or so all over again. Or how much I like to be alone. They don't understand why I have lined a wall with guns that I almost never use. Why I save old boots and hats and hunting clothes. They don't understand that what is just an old coat to them is a memory to me. They see a man who is getting old . . . surrounded by old things. A worn-out-man . . . wearing worn-out boots and covered by a worn-out coat."

He paused to fill his pipe and sat completely still. He made me feel as if I had suddenly, surprisingly, gotten near some wild creature that I didn't want to scare away. But I think, in a way, he had forgotten I was there. He seemed to watch the way the morning clouds were changing shapes and then went on.

"Is there anyone left that could share the meanings of a favorite path along a brook? Or see the time and wind and sun it took to shape a birch tree so exactly right that its shadow in a silent pool is art? I think I could write the words to the song of the goose. The shrill explosive voice of the loon makes my blood remember when someone like me lived in an ancient cave. And when the leaves turn in the autumn it is a signal that a year has passed which I feel was largely lost.

"They don't seem to smell what I smell when the tide comes fresh. They don't listen to the snow or taste the flavors of the wind."

He was about to go on when I felt, more than heard or saw, a pair of teal against the pink of dawn. I turned and shot and scratched one bird down about a hundred yards away. When I got back to the blind he was gone. No evidence that anyone had ever been there except for several burnt-out kitchen matches.

Shortly before lunch the pickup came around to take us back to the lodge. I sat down and looked carefully at every face. I recognized nothing. No one even glanced at me with more than a passing nod. Who was it among us that "no one knew"? Who was it that told me that the sudden, unexpected presence of a deer could make him cry? Who was now hiding behind the ordinary small talk of a duck lodge drink?

I suspected each of them—for a moment. Then none of them; I was almost ready to put it all down as some pre-dawn dream of mine when outside I heard the selfsame voice and through the window I saw a man alone walking toward the marsh. He had just lit a pipe. And thrown the burnt-out wooden match away. For all I know, it could have possibly been you.

NOVEMBER

NOVEMBER IS almost at the end of the road. You start out where it's warm and still in the lingering pause of summer, go through the part where leaves that are left are seared orange and look down into the valley where November lies.

There are many paths in the valley of November. Some lead to the marshes, others to the convoys of bobwhite, or wander to the hardwoods of turkey and whitetail deer.

Follow the dog or let the horse lead the way to where you can just listen for a moment or so and then go softly to where you hear the scratching of the ruffed grouse or the scolding of the squirrels.

Now stop. Wait here a minute or so and look around. There's a sumac where a buck has rubbed the velvet off his horns. Over by the spring you can see the little borings where the woodcock probed for worms; there are still some fox tracks in the mud.

The old chestnut log has lured a drumming grouse for years, the coons that live in the hollow oak nearby have watched him, sleepy-eyed, and somewhat bored. In the clearing, where the farm once was, is a 12-bird covey waiting for the wind to still so they can feed in quiet and keep a watch out for the Coopers hawk.

I know it's hard to wait. The dogs are anxious, the horse frets at the bit, and the boat down by the marsh is bobbing at the line as if it's anxious to get free.

But take just a minute more—you were a long time getting here, you know. Sit still and smell and taste and get the feel of this November.

Soak it up. Go into it softly and thoughtfully, with love and understanding, for another year must pass before you can come this way again. For neither you nor next November will ever be the same.

A HELPING HAND

I'VE GOT a neighbor who's been asking me some questions about shotguns and dogs. Good intelligent questions about the pros and cons of shorthairs, Brittanys, and pointers for our type of cover and birds. Whether I thought that tractability of bitches made up for the problems of having a dog in heat twice a year. How young should the pup be . . . should we consider, if such a dog were ever bought, a professional trainer, etc., etc.

We pretty much settled on the kind of dog that seemed to fit the bill and began to while away the after-dinner hours chit-chatting about shotguns in much the same way.

His wife, getting the solid drift by now, asked me how much a gun costs. So, being—I'll admit—a little cavalier since it wasn't my money, I told her what I'd *like* to be able to pay for a good trap gun, a good skeet gun and a good waterfowl gun *and* a good upland gun. "What in the world does a man need with four different guns?" she asked. I explained that four different guns is merely basic equipment. Only the foundation, so to speak. The barest essentials. I further told her that the average dedicated trapshooter never, never went to a shoot of any size with less than two or three guns and that he probably had twice that number back home. If her husband decided he couldn't really become a *serious* shooter, he would probably enjoy a simple hundred birds or so of skeet per week and wouldn't want more than two or three 12-gauge guns and could get by with just one each in 20, 28, and .410 as companion pieces.

My own wife, who long ago had taken up gardening and sewing in order that the kids could be fed and clothed, remained silent. She knew the truth was what I spoke. She wanted to tell the other woman the fear that trapshooters' wives live with . . . how the addition of a single-barrel model to Winchester's 101 series could wipe out a living room rug for another year or more. That sooner or later every trap gun that has taken root in the family would some time or other be fitted with extra barrels, release triggers and too often, custom-fitted stocks. Not to mention gun cases, shooting glasses in seven shades of color, shell cases, reloading equipment. She wanted to mention six or eight shooting coats—but the sound of Abercrombie & Fitch always brings on a case of migraine. So she remained silent.

As for me, the possibility of luring a new shooter into the purchase of a couple of fine guns acts like a drug. My pupils dilate, my pulse quickens, and my voice takes on a dedicated, missionary timbre. Ahead lies the possibility of selling him one of the guns I'm by now tired of—the dream grows. He buys my *old* guns—I can go out and buy *new* guns. I go on to explain the incredible workmanship in the Krieghoff the way a Methodist minister would quote the Psalms. I quickly have him worshiping at the shrine of the Remington Power-Piston. Parker, Beretta, Fabri, Purdey, Woodward assume the stature of the Apostles.

The moment has passed where cost will ever assume serious mention. He is now my creation . . . a shooter is born.

As he leaves he reminds me for the fiftieth time of my promise to take him to my gun club. His wife refuses to say "goodnight" to me. I shake a drop or two of bitters in my final bourbon; an aura of goodness and satisfaction surrounds me—so much so that I can barely hear my wife murmur "You're a monster . . . a Frankenstein . . . that poor man," and suddenly I realize with shock that I never, even once, mentioned pigeon shooting.

RAIN

SOMEONE ONCE wrote that "rain is the oldest sound to reach the porches of man's ear." I like the sentence and I like the sentiment. And I like rain. I like to hunt in it, fish in it, and just walk around in it. I like the sound of rain, the feel of it and the soft silver look of it. I like the sudden stillness and the change of air with the approach of rain. And the clean-as-a-whistle taste of things just after the rain has stopped.

Like the cold, sleeting rain that laughs at the word *waterproof* (at least as far as anything I own is concerned). This is the kind of rain that makes wildfowlers as eager as puppies. The kind of rain that makes the seat next to the fireplace as good as a throne. The kind of rain that's as good to come in from as it is to go out in. The kind of rain that rattles the shingles to where they sound like a lullaby, if you're a duck hunter, or like the fingernails of a thousand ghosts tapping the windows, if you're not.

Rain makes men sort of huddle together in spirit. I can't remember a hunt in the rain that I didn't enjoy. Especially the soft wetting of the upland woods on the tag end of Indian Summer. That's the kind of a day to gun partridge! The woods are as silent as wet wool, the birds lie good and tight and once you're soaked and get warm again you can understand where they got the phrase "happy as a clam." One of the best shooting days I ever had was with the Coykendalls in a near-flood. We were out after woodcock in early fall and it rained so hard we were soaked to the skin between the front door and the car. Everything was watered down but the whiskey. We changed clothes three times before noon and then said the hell with it and stayed wet.

I do remember that we shot a passel of woodcock, our limit of ducks, and came dangerously close to running out of Angostura bitters. As usual the Labradors loved it and spent the evening steaming themselves in front of the fire languidly stretched out on the piles of wet socks, wet hunting britches, wet sweaters, and wet game coats: all in all giving the room an atmosphere that must have been the olfactory equivalent of the La Brea Tar Pits.

We've hunted together before and we've hunted together since, but the talk always takes on a softer, special tone whenever one of us starts a sentence with "Remember that day in the rain. . . ."

Another of the sporting aspects to rain is the struggle to keep dry. I consider myself the average sportsman when it comes to wet-weather gear and the like. But I have never found anything that goes much higher than my hip boots that really sheds water except a real rubber parka which I have but don't like because I sweat so much I might as well get wet from the rain. I'm a great fan of hip boots and I might as well admit that I used to go out of my way to look for excuses to wear them—especially in the days when four-pound boots only weighed two pounds—but now that four-pound boots weigh in at eight to ten, I tend to give the issue some second thinking.

I grew up with a hunting friend of my father's who settled on the other extreme. Whenever it was wet or snowy he wore sneakers, no socks, just high-top sneakers. His theory was that you got wet feet anyway so why postpone the inevitable. He scorned gloves under the same principle and yet I swear I never heard him once complain about being cold or wet.

At the other extreme I once saw a friend of mine put on *nine* layers of clothes—all he had and half of mine—in an effort to fend off a North Carolina sleet storm. He was so bulky the guide and I had to lay him in the back seat of the car like a fence post. By the time we'd walked the mile or so to the goose blind he was wringing wet with sweat from the inside and rain from the outside. It took about an hour for all this to freeze together as we predicted. As he collected more and more water he got heavier and heavier until we thought he'd just fall through the bottom of the blind, from where nothing less than a tractor could have budged him.

On the way back he walked like a mechanical monster. I was so surprised he could move at all, I said nothing but encouraging words among cautions about where to put his feet. We were scared to death he might stumble and fall. I could picture him lying helpless on the ground like some mired mastodon in camouflage threshing about in the mud. The only way we could have moved him was to have each grabbed an arm and dragged him along like a huge log. We finally made it back; slung him in the car again like a dressed beef and started off. As he lay there gasping, all he could do was list the stuff he planned to buy to wear for next time—in addition to what he had on right now!

You'll have to admit that one of the nicest things about getting wet is getting dry. How about the feeling of sticking your feet into some nice warm, dry sheepskin slippers! A fresh, clean shirt and britches and snuggle your backside up in front of the fire—if you can move the dogs out of your way.

Then you warm a quart of milk, add a pint or so of bourbon whiskey, a few teaspoons of sugar, a couple of drops of vanilla, a clove or two, a sprinkle of nutmeg. Divide this equally amongst those tossed by the storms.

Now, if you'll excuse me I'll go dig out my old tweed hat, my ducking coat, and rubber boots. I'm going to get one of the dogs for an excuse to go for a little evening walk. I might even have to turn my pipe upside down—it seems as if it's starting to rain.

A WINDOW ON THE POND

I SIT and work—or call it that—in a little room I have; far enough removed from the house to be out of hearing range of my wife and two daughters. That's a big advantage, but not the only one. There's a seven-foot window that overlooks a swampy meadow that someday will be a mini-lake for me. I intend to build a set of wood duck houses on the farthest shore so I can watch them come and go and raise their young. I'll raise a dozen mallards there to keep me company, and hopefully a pair of geese. Some largemouth bass, catfish, and bluegills will be stocked so I can teach my kids to fish.

There's something about a small pond that stirs me deeply. If there was a national contest to see who could just sit and watch a tiny pond—you could put your bets on me. I've got my binoculars up on the windowsill all set to go to work. And "work" is what a man does when he watches his own pond. There'll be snappers in there that I'll have to shoot to save my baby ducks, and run water-snake patrols so they won't eat too many frogs.

One problem that I've got to face is owls. We have some great horned owls living right nearby in my huge sycamore. I do love owls and I'm sure that owls love tender little ducks. Or will the ducks go under cover in a wire pen at night—and will the owls restrict their hunting to a sportive nighttime schedule? We shall see.

Planning a pond is more fun than having a Sears, Roebuck catalogue just to read. Choosing water lilies, and some other plants to feed the ducks will take us weeks, and all along the shore I'm going to plant a random mess of trees just because I like the way they look. Birches, willows, dawn redwoods, and sugar maples and one or two dwarf apple trees so I'll have food come fall, and right there in my hand so I won't have to leave if I don't want to.

I hope my Labradors will keep the muskrats out. I hate to have them burrowing under all the banks and making holes to catch me in my rounds.

But, back to the room. Three-foot heaps of magazines I like to save. And lots of books—writing is the best excuse I know to sneak away and read. Pictures of hunting buddies hang on every wall and dogs that I've been owned by all stare back at me from faded black and white snapshots taken in some long lost cover that probably supports a house or two by now. As soon as I can get some extra old-time decoys—out they'll come. There's a small fireplace out here, and a threadbare scrap of rug my dogs sleep on while they pretend to watch me work and a nice soft cot for me to stretch out on so I can think! So far, I haven't woken up at three or four A.M. and had to sneak back into the other house. But I think I'll make a note to get an alarm clock—just in case. I want an old junk shotgun to make a standing lamp and a next-to-worthless refrigerator to keep cold beer in. That should keep me out here long enough to really get some writing done. I don't know how all the other writers work but the word that suits me pretty close is *lazy*. I'll spend two hours cleaning out my briar pipes, re-loading shotgun shells, re-reading magazines, and doing nothing but staring out at clouds. If I kept my guns out here to clean and fiddle with I'd never get a damn thing done.

But all in all, it's a good room for a mid-winter dreamer. A room to put hunting buddies up in—where we sit and look at pictures of shots we'll never have again, in places we might never go again, and stare at faces of men we've known and liked and will never again see. They are gone with their dogs; Beau and Tick and

Fly and Little Ben and Belle—and they took too much of the good times with them.

It's a room to sit alone in when that time comes when I must be by myself and think about my friends; the dogs they dreamed of hunting over and the guns they wished they owned. Some folks say that's wasting time, but it's nice to have an old time tale or laugh—or lie—come back in mid-winter, still alive from a great October day that's long lost to every other living soul—but you and me.

A MOLE AND A MOUSE

A FRIEND of mine told me that an old wrangler in Montana had expressed it best when he said "the thing that a man hunts when he hunts is himself." I don't know when I've heard it put better. I know I have to "hunt myself" because I "lose myself" so often. When things get to the point that I don't like where I am, what I'm doing, or how I'm acting—it's time to whistle up the dogs and get away. I, as often as not, enjoy the day when nothing happens, like a nothing day I spent on a deer stand. The sun was just warm enough to put me in a slight doze and in the midst of dreaming the great dream I felt aware of some activity involving the bottom of my leather-top rubbers. I peeked down and saw a field mouse nibbling at the sole of my boot. He seemed like a friendly fellow and I felt like having company so I stayed stock still and pleasured myself watching him, until a scolding bluejay made me jump and I frightened him away. And somehow, I'm not sure why, but this seemed to put the right perspective on everything for me for a while. Maybe as simple as the realization that a lot of things in life have a tougher row to hoe than I do.

We all have those times when we just plain don't understand anything about anything. When life seems curiously meaningless and cruelty and unhappiness have become common companions to us, then the woods can offer us special sanctuary. The sight of a suckling fawn or a hen partridge fussing over her chicks can tell us a lot about love and faith. There is an order, a proper scheme of things in the wild that I find reassuring. The perspective felt by a small, middle-aged man wandering beneath towering trees that have seen centuries is good for me. To be cussed out by a bluejay from above and nibbled at by a mouse from below can do a lot to strip away the silly self-importance we carry for no good reason. I have neither the survival instinct of the mouse, nor the courage of the jay. I can't burrow very well and I certainly can't fly. I am just an object of curiosity that moves in a cumbersome way and whose odor is offensive and frightening to most wild things. I don't smell very well, my hearing is nothing to that possessed by the deer, and my eyes are almost useless compared to the birds. My hide can't keep me warm and to defend myself against attack, using only my bare hands, would be pathetic in consequence.

A four-ounce mole is 100 times stronger for his size than I am and his bravery is monumental. Compared to even the smallest of beings I am some kind of biological oddity who depends for his survival on the complexities of a self-made social order. I don't mind being ordered about by a jay—after all it is his house that I'm smelling up and stumbling through. So I'll go back where I belong, knowing that the absolute truth about me is that my species must function around the fact that compared to most of the living things in the world we are pitiful creatures.

I have "hunted myself" and I have found myself. I must admit I'd make a damn poor trophy.

TELLING LIES

AFTER I'D been out shooting chukar partridge with Larry Dino-vitz, the head man of the Rocking *K* Ranch in Bishop, California, we got together over what the cowboys used to call "tongue oil." And as things got along in conversation, Larry got to telling lies about his Labrador, Charlie. And I got to telling lies about my Labradors, Tippy and Judy. Larry, being a gentleman at heart, started out easy with half-mile retrieves and I countered with three-quarter-mile retrieves—on doubles. Then Larry mentioned that Charlie's work on these half-mile retrieves was on giant Canada geese and I added that my three-quarter milers were through a couple of inches of ice. Well, Larry's dog got going nearer and nearer to Alaska and mine got to plowing through stuff that the Coast Guard icebreaker *Eastwind* would flinch at and we started to call it a draw. Larry mixed another batch and suddenly Charlie rose up from under Larry's feet behind the bar and started to bark. Larry said, with a straight face, that Charlie was pretty good at mixing drinks and was reminding him that he had forgotten to add the Triple Sec to the Margueritas. I didn't say anything, Larry being the host, but I really don't believe that *any* Labrador retriever can tell the difference between Triple Sec and Cointreau. Even mine.

"TROUBLE"

WE LOST a little puppy the other day to a speeding car. And a lot of the magic has disappeared from the kitchen where she ruled the roost. Whoever said "you can't buy happiness" forgot little puppies. "Trouble" was a tiny package crammed to overflowing with mischief, charm, excitement, curiosity, and affection. She scattered love around our house the way the wind scatters leaves. The empty voids in space are not one whit more vast than the little corner by the stove where the puppy slept—when the puppy's sleeping somewhere else forever.

OLD TOM

THE VET told him that the old setter might live another day or so and that the humane thing to do would be to put him down. The old man brushed his moustache with the back of his hand so that his fingers would cover up his eyes and said he didn't believe he was ready to do without Old Tom right now. Maybe in a day or so, but not right now.

So the two of them shuffled out to the car and drove off together. Now the old man had a problem. It was the middle of March and bird season was long since closed. But more than he'd ever wanted anything in his life he wanted the dog to hear one more shot and feel the whirr of one more flush.

March or no, the old man took a vigil near the swamp that night and marked down two or three birds as they came in to roost. And promptly at six the next morning the two gentlemen marched down together through the morning mist, as they had done countless times before . . . and as one of them hoped they would do countless times again in some other fields.

The play was faultless. Old Tom drew himself up as proud as a puppy. The old man's shot was as true as a youngster's and the deed was done.

At the vet's a half-hour later, his last bird cradled between his front feet, his nostrils filled with the scent of what he had lived for, Old Tom went to sleep.

The old man lets him rest up on a hillside facing the western sun . . . old folks appreciate the late afternoon warmth. And on the slate that marks the spot he scratched *"Old Tom. A faithful friend for 12 fine years."* On fair days, when he thinks no one is watching, the old man goes up to the slate on the hillside and sits in the sun with a glass of whiskey and talks about times past with Tom.

TRAINING CHILDREN

THERE'S A phenomenon in nature that the scientists call "imprinting." Imprinting is more or less a natural instinct in an animal that can be made to go wrong—or can be effected artificially. For example, when a young duckling chirps for food and your hand appears with some mash or grain the duckling assumes that you are its mother and begins to follow you around. Animals can be artificially reared and imprinted with less difficulty than is generally supposed. I think that anyone who was raised on a farm can remember the duck that was raised by a chicken and grew up believing he was a chicken. I have a cat that was raised, including nursing, by an English setter and that cat today thinks she's a dog. As a matter of fact my other dogs more or less treat her as an equal and one of the few things she really doesn't like is another cat.

I might have had some sort of long-forgotten imprinting by a trapshooter, since I continue to think I'm one in spite of about 20 reasons out of every 25 that prove to the contrary. But why couldn't we do this really with our children and breed a generation who would sneer at anyone without the ability to go 500 straight? What would happen if you took your infant son or daughter and tried a little experiment? Suppose every time the baby cried for food you let it watch you smash a clay target and then fed the child. As the child got a little stronger you taught it that when it wanted food all it had to do was break a White Flyer and it got some delicious whipped prunes or minced chicken gizzards. It would soon learn that a broken clay meant affection and goodies. The next step would be some kind of advancement in skill. You would slide the target across the front of the high chair and make the child break it with a spoon as it passed by. If it missed—no mashed potatoes.

Before long, by natural progression in degrees of difficulty, you would have a nine-year-old who could go 25 straight with a .410 from 10 yards. By the time he or she was big enough to handle your Winchester it would be a matter of ripping off 100 straight before breakfast! All this to be done in the utmost secrecy, needless to say. I figure, conservatively, that with the unveiling of your prodigy at the Grand American in Vandalia, Ohio, you would be standing on the threshold of at least $15,000 in purses. With this money you can start that little business you've been dreaming about and retire, a well-heeled gentlemen of leisure, shortly before you're 35. Please don't forget who gave you the idea. The editorial offices will forward all checks.

HOGGING UP

RIGHT NOW I'm tying a mental red ribbon around my annual Christmas present to myself—a few days down the Eastern Shore, along the edges of Chesapeake Bay. Some say I drift down there just for the crab cakes. Others maintain just as stoutly that the purpose of the trip is either the buffet at the Tidewater Inn or the Fishing Bay oysters. I admit, in part, that everyone of my spokesmen has a point well taken, but I really go to see the geese. I admit to the cherished but futile dream that I'll run across an old swan decoy or a set of Mason factory black duck blocks, and I'll admit that I *do* spend some time bumming around boat yards and general stores. I like to talk to the old baymen. The old market gunners. The boat builders. They're a great source of information, not all of it gospel truth, but interesting just the same.

For instance, I'll bet you never heard of "cringing an oyster." This is a little trick I learned from Paul Mills, a fine professional shooting guide. You start with a glass of whiskey—bourbon to be sure. Then you shuck an oyster and drop him in the glass of whiskey—and watch him *cringe*. That's exactly what he does; kind of curls up. Then with your fingers or pocket knife, depending on what kind of a sport you are, you pick him up and eat him! I don't know the chemistry of it all, but I do know that something happens to the oyster and it's good!

But, as I said, I really go there to watch the geese.

And I've discovered that the best cook I know there soaks his ducks and geese overnight in skimmed milk before he roasts them; if that's the secret of the best waterfowl I ever ate . . . the world should know about it.

I know where the best crabcakes are made (10 cents apiece; a lot of crab meat with a touch of bread packing). And if you don't eat at least two bowls of snapper soup (made from freshwater snapping turtles) at the Tidewater Inn every day, a lot of the trip is wasted. I will not discuss fresh crabs covered with black pepper, fried Chincoteague oysters, or homemade pecan pie. After all, we're here in Maryland to bring home Canadian geese. Hush puppies, grits, red-eye gravy, and sugar-cured ham are just the bare necessities; the staples of day-to-day existence. When you go shooting half the fun is roughing it, right? The fact that at a certain shooting club I know you're welcomed back at eight or so in the morning, after you've gunned the early flights, with a secret formula milk punch that could very well have been the fabled nectar of the gods, and eggs poached in white wine, doesn't mean that the sport has gone all-to-hell and you with it, does it? And what harm is there in getting around some breast of duck sauteed in brandy and Cointreau and orange bitters? It sure beats stale cheese sandwiches. (After a couple of days of leftovers along the Eastern Shore even my Labrador won't eat stale cheese sandwiches!)

This year, while I'm down there to watch the geese, I'll make a survey of the victuals taken out to the blinds where life is earnest and the Northeast wind has a bite like a wolf. I don't believe you'd think you stumbled into a church picnic . . . Here is one of the few places in America where you can gun and rest assured that all the talk about magnums isn't completely referring to shotguns! I can just imagine two men sitting in a blind discussing the contents of their Thermos bottles. One would turn to the other and say "Oh, I think a nice white wine is fine for shooting quail or partridge, but for ducks and geese I'll stick with Jack Daniel's or Wild Turkey."

FATE

A FAMOUS historian once remarked to the effect that "experience gives us the ability to act with foresight." Now, as a public service I would like to pass on some general observations to you, from my experience, so that you can act with foresight. Experiences like these are in many ways superior to fact. For example, if you wanted to know the proper amount of powder to use for loading match cartridges for a .30-06 you would straight off drop a note to Elmer Keith or the like. You would receive a factual answer. That is pure knowledge and you have shrewdly gone to the right source. But wisdom is a broader thing and you are at the source of some of it right now. And I trust that you will sense with compassion that wisdom is too frequently purchased with hardship and suffering.

To wit: Never hunt with a man who doesn't carry a game bag.

Never eat at a place called *"Mom's."*

If you find a hunting coat you really like, buy two, because if it's any good they'll quit making it.

Brag about your dog after the hunt—not before.

Never marry a woman who doesn't know how to pick ducks.

Never lend your gun to a man you're shooting against.

If you borrow a friend's dog to take woodcock shooting, blindfold him coming and going.

Never shoot leadoff at trap or skeet.

Keep an eye on the man who carries two compasses. He'll get lost.

Never tell your wife how much guns, dogs, or gun clubs really cost.

Never forget that most streams are one inch higher than most hip boots.

Barbed wire is always an inch lower than you bend.

The extremely well-dressed stranger with the fancy guns will turn out to have an AA average at skeet.

The wind will always blow a gale when you shoot, and die down when you're through.

When the birds are divided after the hunt, yours will have the most shot.

The list is virtually endless—and virtually predictable. If I were a gambling man I'd give odds and make money. But somehow, for the likes of us, wisdom is always tempered by enthusiastic wishful thinking. We believe that it will be the club champion's firing pin that will break, not ours.

But the thing that saves us is probably the fact that deep down inside we really don't care all that much. The happiest days are really those tempered by a pinch of fate. If we mistake the salt for the sugar it'll just be something to remember with a smile. Tomorrow's another day and maybe the Lord really will temper the wind on the shorn.

A FISHING NUT

I HAVE a friend who's such a nut about fishing that he almost always manages to refer to the incidents in his life in angling terms of a sort. I met him for lunch the other day after a long, hard walk through a driving rain and arrived at the table with my hair all wet and my clothes in a pretty rough array. He took a prolonged look at me, searching for exactly the right phrase, shook his head in sympathy and said, "Gene, you look just like a badly tied fly."

A CHRISTMAS STORY

CHRISTMAS IS bitter-sweet. The quiet sanctity of the season has long been bludgeoned by marketing, and the longed-for gentle quiet never seems to come.

It's hard not to turn cynic and say "Times ain't what they used to be." And you might well hear someone say back to you. "They never were!"

I think a lot of us would like to spend part of December in our own kind of cathedral. A taut-drawn tent in a mountain pass. A spot down South where the evening carols would be the calling of quail. Or right there at timberline where the bugling of elk can pass for golden trumpets. Or that little brook you know where you can just listen to silence, while an inquisitive field mouse nibbles at the toe of your boot.

I think we know where our kind of Christmas really is. No man-made, plastic-covered, ribbon-wrapped joy is going to fill the bill. Christmas, as one man said so well, "is inside us."

I guess I'm saying that we have to run away from what is beginning to pass as festivity to find where the real festival is. Not a return to the age of innocence, but a return to the wonder of the mystery that we will never understand. Not to the answer of the computer, but to the asking of *The Question*.

My kind of Christmas week would involve me completely; a lot of it would be spent in my old clothes and sheepskin slippers.

It would start two or three days before Christmas, if I could set it up the way I want. The way I really want. The weather would be clear and cold, with the smell and feel of a coming snow hanging heavily in the air. My family, my wife and two little girls, would pack up the gear in our aging station wagon and point the nose toward the nor'east weather. At journey's end would be an old, but snug cabin. Preferably one made out of slab pine still heavy with bark. The fieldstone fireplace would cradle a four-foot log and a big window would face West toward the setting of the sun.

A half-mile or so away would be a duck blind set on a sheltered cove, a good sturdy blind that dulled the edge of the wind at your back, had room for a charcoal stove made out of a five-gallon pail, with some marsh hay piles up in one corner for the Labradors to sit up on, because they love to look out swivelheaded, for the passing birds.

We'd go out, all of us, little girls and all, to gun the morning flight. Then back for breakfast. Homemade country sausage patties, fried eggs, hominy grits, and black coffee (with a touch of rum in it for the father).

Then break out the sled for a trip for wood. The little hands at work for branch-kindling while I enjoy the chore of splitting wood. Remember the just-released smell of oak and pine, the smell that just comes twice, once as the ax cleaves the log—and again if the fire is precisely right and your logs have had some chance to dry.

To close the day, just the dogs and I go out alone to watch the evening sun sink, somehow without a steamy hiss, into the outer arm of water beyond our hook of beach.

After supper, while the dishes are getting done, the Labradors busy themselves supervising over my cleaning of the guns and setting up the stuff for dressing in the cold velvet dark of tomorrow morning.

And then we read. Aloud. Jack London's, "To Build a Fire" or from his *The Call of the Wild*. Or Kenneth Grahame's *The*

Wind in the Willows. Or a piece of that incredible *Once and Future King* by the late T. H. White. Then the special deep and sweetest sleep that can only come to the dreamer who lies beneath a six-inch comforter of down.

So the few days would go. Popping corn. Making candy. Or maple sugar icicles from the trees outside. Snow balls, flavored with vanilla and sugar. Chewing teaberry and sassafras bark. Whistle making or building a hearth broom out of rushes. Simple things; not necessary in our times. But just for the touch of it. Just for knowing that it once was done for need and the pleasure of being someone who still knows how.

And reading snow. Following the lace-making of mice feet. The mysterious arrival and disappearance of the tracks of partridge or pheasant. The parallel exclamation points left by some wandering buck or doe. The tiny, nearly human, delicate handprints of the coons or sleepless possums. The business-like, heavy, working footprint of the never-resting muskrat. The spade-like paddle print of ducks.

I don't know when a man can be busier doing nothing than when in a winter-quiet camp. Shoring up the nest against the impersonal cold of December when instinct sends everything else toward a warmer sun or below the frozen deck to a dark sleep; not awakened by less than starvation hunger, to drowse and rumble until a softened pre-spring wind makes the waking welcome.

If I had my way it would storm all Christmas Eve. Lacking, to my sorrow, a horse and cutter with bells on to skim through the whispering fall of snow, I would put myself in harness and with the little guys behind on a sled we would go out and decorate a Christmas tree.

One of the stories I like to tell is how some trees became evergreens. The one that tells how anxious they were to protect the small animals and birds. And we will find a small spruce or fir and hang suet from its palms. Some other, older, pine will have some branches stripped for the smell of Christmas as we put it on the fire back at camp.

Then the gifts. I have a seven-year old girl who wants a knife. To carve with. You think she'll cut herself? I think so too. I know I did with my first knife, but that will heal and she will learn. And learn to carve. Do you know a better way of telling someone young "I trust you?"

The other little girl would like a duck call. Lord knows why. I think partly because she's a kind of noisy cuss who likes the voice of geese and ducks and partly because she knows the Labradors enjoy the raucous quacks. Can you imagine the kind of sound a baby moose with wings would make? However . . . this is Christmas Eve.

In one corner, in the firelight, a small pile of white pine shavings grow. From the other, the guttural honks of some undreamed of bird. And outside the snow is making a halo of light to be seen through the window. I give a silent toast to whoever it was that discovered, or invented, bourbon, little girls, Labrador retrievers, duck calls, wives and whittling knives, and you know that right now I am in the presence of contentment.

HOW TO WIN

I HAD lunch with Rudy Etchen the other day and it was a most enjoyable occasion for two reasons: one is the fact that Rudy bought and the other is the fact that he is probably one of the three or four finest shotgun handlers in the world . . . and on too many days to count has been proved the best of the best. Rudy's knowledge of the shotgun is so incredibly profound as to be embarrassing to me, so I stayed on more familiar ground and asked him a more pertinent question. "What makes a shooter great?" (All this, you realize, is part of my search for the Holy Grail—how to improve my own shooting without endless hours of prayer and practice.)

Rudy thought a moment and said "A great shooter just will not lose." Think about that for a minute; I did. And then I asked him the obvious question.

"But they do lose—you beat them and on occasions they beat you."

"No," Rudy answered as if speaking to a very small and slow-witted child, "You don't understand, the only person that ever beat me was myself." I nodded in vague agreement. "Given a certain degree of skill and the properly fitted gun for the game you have 20 percent of the 100 percent needed to make a fine shooter. The other 80 percent is concentration. And concentration is self-belief. Self-belief makes the shooter great."

Is shooting a question of will? Is it like that achievement of the four-minute mile? I think it is. We all have days when we will not be denied—but the likes of us know that the likes of Rudy Etchen will have a great deal many more of them. And there, in that last sentence is the summation of why, if I am ever shooting with Rudy, you will notice that my sentimental attachment for my bank account will forbid any friendly fivers from being wagered on the result. Rudy will win. Why, I even let him beat me to the lunch check.

CULTURE

THERE ISN'T generally much pure, 24–carat culture to be gleaned from this monthly page—nor, in truth, from the lightly lettered man who writes it. I get my culture from the same place you get yours.

So, having gotten that modest burden off my chest, we will ascend to our betters—or at least mine. One of the strange anomalies about outdoor writing is that there is at one and the same time, so much of it and so little of it. It seems that a lot of men write about it in some very fine books and no one, compared to the readership of the trash that too frequently rises to the best-seller category, reads it.

This was brought to mind the other day when I was chatting with an old friend of mine, William P. Fox. Now, Bill is a professional writer of fiction and semi-fiction, and some articles which he claims to be factual. Bill wrote a collection of short stories a few years back called *Southern Fried*. It was funny, beautifully written, and deservedly well-praised by the critics.

One thing led to another and Bill ended up teaching at a college in Iowa. He met an associate of his named Vance Bourjaily who has been introducing Bill to the joys of the hunting field. Now, as you probably know, Mr. Bourjaily is a nationally known novelist of the first rank. Anyone who claims to be a student of American fiction knows of him.

So, to get back to the point, I asked Bill Fox if he'd enjoyed Bourjaily's book on hunting as much as I did. Bill said "Vance never did a book on hunting."

I said, "He wrote what should be a classic in its field called *The Unnatural Enemy*." Bill said he'd be damned and I agreed that he should be unless he got hold of the book, read it, and paid his compliments to the author as well as my personal respects.

Now, since most of the hunters that I know can read and write at least enough to use a mail-order catalogue, why is it that all this good stuff is carefully avoided by all but a handful of the 50 million or more folks who like a lot of their pleasures in the open air?

One problem is that books of this nature—according to the publishers—don't sell. So, naturally the publishers don't advertise them. Sort of like the snake swallowing its own tail. So that creates the cycle. The publishers won't advertise, the bookstores won't stock, and most of us never know that they exist. And the book shortly goes out of print. Years later when it has become a "classic" to nuts like me who collect them, the original price has gone up six-fold—or more.

I was recently offered $60 for a copy of *New England Grouse Shooting* that I paid about $4 for. It originally sold for $10, but since no one bought it, it went on sale and our little cycle happened again. I'd be willing to bet that even Vance Bourjaily never heard of it. Or of the man who wrote it. William H. Foster, who among other things—was not only a superb illustrator, but happened to be the man who invented skeet shooting.

Now that I'm on the verge again of being circuitous and long-winded, I'll surprise you by coming to the point. Maybe. Since we're kind of between hunting seasons and our womenfolk have us out gallivanting here and there, I'll give you something to look for in bookstores, antique shops, or from a neighbor's library. A list of old and new friends you may not have known you have: The *Tranquillity* series by Sheldon, three volumes. *Seven Grand Gun Dogs* by Ray Holland. *Stories from Under the Sky* by John

Madson. Any book by Ed Zern. Burton Spiller's *Grouse Feathers,*
Firelight, or *More Grouse Feathers.* Theodore Roosevelt's *African*
Game Trails. Any book by John Taintor Foote, or Archibald
Rutledge. And keep an eye out for *The Voice of Bugle Ann,* by
MacKinlay Kantor. Of course, *The Green Hills of Africa* by
Ernest Hemingway. I don't know of nicer companions to spend an
evening with.

And, while we're on the subject, there's a book out called *An*
Exultation of Larks; that being the old name for a flock of the
birds—like a covey of quail or a flight of ducks. All these tempt-
ingly lead us into inventing our own. How about an *apology* of
trapshooters? Or a *numb* of duck hunters . . . a *fib* of fisher-
men. A *stumbling* of coonhunters. A *stammer* of bourbon fanciers.
Or a *frown* of editors. A *shriek* of wives. Kind of fun, isn't it? Go
ahead, try some, it'll help pass the time in the blind between flights.
Just one more and I'll quit: an *exaggeration* of guides.

LOG FIRES

THERE ARE few things most outdoor-minded men pride themselves on more than the ability to build a good fire.

I know I can start with a match, a nice dry chestnut log and a hatchet and bring a quart bucket of cold water to a rolling boil in less than five minutes. This particular accomplishment will not be whispered about in awed tones by my pals, but I take great pleasure in the fact. I think you can tell a lot about a man in the way he behaves around a fire—at home by the fireplace, in a gunning lodge, or the best of all fires—by the edge of a lake with only the wild voiced loons for company. They used to say that if you wanted to draw a crowd, start mixing a martini and suddenly six people would show up and tell you how to do it. But log fires are worse. People are forever poking and messing around with my fires; and never doing much good. I belong to the "start it right and leave it pretty much alone" school. I've just about gotten to the point where I hide my fireplace tools to keep meddlers from fussing around with a perfectly fine fire. To me a good fire doesn't roar and flame. It's obedient and thoughtful. It just burns quietly to provide a little background color to the stories and fill up the lulls in the conversation.

Ever notice how much the hunting dogs love a fire with their menfolk sitting around? Old Tip, my lovely lady Labrador, will snuggle up to a scorcher until I'll swear I can smell her singe. She'll toast one side, then the other. More often than not, when bedtime comes around she looks the other way or pretends she's deep in sleep because she wants to spend the night alone staring at the coals. Good fires make good friends.

And here's an old verse about wood that I've always wanted to memorize and never will:

> Beechwood fires are bright and clear
> If the logs are kept a year.
> Chestnut's only good, they say,
> If for long it's laid away.
> Birch and fir logs burn too fast,
> Blaze up bright and do not last.
> Elm wood burns like a churchyard mold;
> Even the very flames are cold.
> Poplar gives a bitter smoke,
> Fills your eyes and makes you choke.
> Apple wood will scent your room
> With an incense like perfume.
> Oak and maple, if dry and old,
> Keep away the winter cold.
> But ash wood wet and ash wood dry,
> A king shall warm his slippers by.

KEEPING WARM

IN THE process of exchanging winter clothes for summer clothes in the storeroom in the attic I luckily ran across some old hunting clothes that gave me an excuse to sit down and wool gather (no pun intended) about the days before there were insulated boots and underwear.

Some things are better. It is a lot easier to spray your hunting shirts with some silicone waterproofing than to concoct a smelly mess of beeswax and paraffin to dip stuff in. I was of the school that would rather get soaked than walk around smelling like the inside of a lamp chimney. But the biggest and the best arguments were on how to keep warm. There was the "layer of newspapers" school, where the weekly paper was tied around your body underneath the next to last shirt. You could hear who opted that way. Then there was always one tough-skinned old badger who just wore one, that's right, just *one* heavy wool shirt—mind you the weather often got down to zero and at 5 or 6 o'clock A.M. it was often far below. The "Mother's School" is the one I guess I got trapped in—both figuratively and literally. Mothers didn't want to see any skin showing, except maybe a little around the eyes. You wore everything you could stagger under and that was topped off with bib overalls that were cut-downs of your father's. After a half hour of walking, say to a deer stand, you were soaked through with sweat and promptly froze. You could not, however, convince your mother of this fact and consequently a boy risked pneumonia all winter long until he got big enough to win the argument, or tough enough to take four or five layers off and stand the consequences when he was found out—which he always was. Another problem, social as well as thermal, was whether or not it was "sissy" to wear the ear flaps down. We all had caps that were usually corduroy with ear flaps that tied at the top in a bow knot, letting the flaps loosely caress your frozen ears, but no torture on earth could have persuaded me to appear in a deer gang with the knot tied underneath my chin! Mittens of various materials: buckskin, or best of all a heavy homemade yarn, or all kinds of gloves. None of which ever worked to my certain memory. You simply walked around with your hands in your pockets as much as you could. I don't remember anyone who escaped a touch of frostbite on at least one of two fingers.

I guess that originality and conviction really started out at the bottom—with the feet. Erd Reeves either wore sneakers—in two or three feet of snow: all day long—or a tattered pair of hip boots with no socks. Did his feet ever freeze? No. But I have no idea why not. No idea at all. The local loggers wore their stupid knee high, tight laced leather boots that not only cut off most of the circulation but were instantly wet and unbearably cold. But I must admit I envied the dashing appearance they made and I'm sure I made out more than one imaginary order to Sears for a pair just in case I ever got the money; which luckily I never did.

Outside all this variety was some sort of coat so you'd have pockets available. Nine out of ten wore near identical faded blue denim farm coats that smelled of sweet Holsteins or Jerseys. If you had the money—and it wasn't too much in those days, unless you didn't have it, which was the rule—you bought a red and black plaid Woolrich hunting coat with its magnificent high collar. I never could afford one, and by the time a friend of my father's wore his out to where he'd got a new one and passed the old one down to me, I was too long in the arms to wear it.

We may have looked and smelled funny, stuffed with paper and crammed into the bib overalls until they stretched tight like homemade sausage casings, but the reasons for being out are still the same. And the arguments about what to wear still go on. But now, when the weather nudges bottom, I stand patiently in the kitchen and wait until my wife's more nimble fingers have tied the ear flaps underneath my chin.

THE WOODCOCK LETTER

Dear Marcia:

I suppose you and the kids have been wondering what happened to me since the night, a week ago, when I went out to get whiskey. And I suppose my office has been bothering you about my absence.

Well, the answer as to where I've been—and still am—is simple, but the reasons why I am here are somewhat hard to follow. So, please be patient and try.

You remember kidding me about having six or eight books on woodcock on my bed table and how it seemed to you I read about practically nothing else? And how you remarked that the only way I'd get to know more about the bird than I already know would be to talk to one?

Well, as I was going up the lane in the car my headlights picked up a woodcock feeding along the side of the road. He (perhaps she; you'll recall how I told you about the difficulty of telling the sexes apart—and how the female is generally slightly larger and the bill slightly longer . . .) seemed much less shy than I anticipated. So boldened by curiosity, I stopped the car and very slowly and quietly got out of the front seat and walked within a few feet of the bird. He had stopped feeding and was peering at me—his huge soft brown eyes glittering like amber diamonds in the reflected light from the car. More for fun than anything else, I went "peent . . . peent" or at least attempted what I thought a woodcock would sound like. He seemed only slightly astonished that I would make an effort to communicate with him and after only a moment's hesitation, he too went "peent . . . peent."

Now I have never heard of a wild game bird making any effort to communicate with man, but here, clearly, was a creature who understood me. Suddenly I remembered that the little belt can of fish worms was still in the back seat of the car and stealthily I glided around the car to where I could reach down and get it. I picked out a worm and tossed it softly near him. He stepped over and tucked it away as if I'd been feeding him for years.

Clearly we had some sort of understanding going on. My mind raced through several possibilities. Should I try to capture and tame him? Should I see if we could establish some kind of talk right now . . . or should I quit this moment and go about my business and let him go on about his? Then he made up my mind for me. Ever since I had given him the worm, he had been staring at me in a rather curious fashion—almost as if he could read my thoughts. He had apparently noticed where the worm had come from and with a few very stately hops he was in the back seat of the car probing busily in my bait can. In a moment or two he had gobbled the contents and seemed full. He regarded me in a rather friendly fashion once more and then seemed to settle himself down in my fishing shirt and looked as though he wished to take a little nap.

I climbed in the car, softly closed the door and started down the driveway—I wasn't really sure where I was going to go but I felt an urgency to move south toward the rising moon.

As the car moved on a few miles, the little fellow in the back seat awoke and hopped up on the dash board in front of me and watched the proceedings. It wasn't too long until I had a feeling that he understood what was happening. He began to march nervously back and forth over the part of the dash where the clock is and tap his bill on the windshield as though to indicate the direction he wanted us to follow. As soon as I determined this—or thought I had—I began to leave the highway and found myself following a zig-zag series of long neglected country roads. And, as it was when we began, in front of us I could always see the ascending moon. Now and then, the woodcock would give voice to a mild "peent . . . peent." Not so much a call as it was the voicing of a thing well done. He seemed to be saying "yes . . . yes . . ." as the car veered from one unknown road to another. As we journeyed through the night he seemed alert and cheerful. Someone who knew what he was doing and the best way to get the job done.

However, as the morning sun arose it seemed to depress him. He seemed less sure of our direction and, if not disinterested, at least not terribly concerned. As for myself, I was, as you may have guessed, getting more than a little tired. Finally we got to the point, somewhere near Cape May County, New Jersey, of mutual exhaustion. I pulled the car off the log road we'd been traveling, and fell asleep.

When I awoke it was to the insistent summons of my traveling companion, tapping on the windshield and pacing back and forth, eager to step outside in the gathering dusk. It was with some questioning of myself that I opened the door and watched him flutter past my face into the nearby meadow. But the nonchalance of his exit and the brevity of his flight gave me some reassurance that our acquaintance had taken some deep rooting in the past few hours.

I followed him out and decided that I'd give him a hand and turned-to-rolling over some nearby stones and tossing the earthworms I found in his direction. He accepted them gratefully. After 15 or 20 worms had been swallowed he staggered contentedly toward the car, popped himself back up on the dashboard and signaled me to get moving.

That, in brief, Marcia and my beloved children, is what happened. The events of the first day's journey have been repeated time and again and I suspect we are headed for some spot in Louisiana where he intends to spend the winter. Our conversations have been mutually informative and a deep friendship has developed—far enough so that on more than one day's journey I have had several of his acquaintances traveling with us. Those too old or tired, from the looks of them, to do it all alone on wing.

I must apologize for the undue worry and concern I have caused you all at home and in the office; but I trust you understand

the uniqueness of my journey. And, if you do not fully compre-
hend how I feel about it, I know that you are at least sympathetic
to my emotions.

Trusting all is well, I again apologize. We are nearing the end
of our journey and I believe I will be able to start homeward in less
than a week from today.

My love to all,
Gene

THE 3-BIRD ACCIDENT

A SHOOTING buddy of mine, Dave George, who is an absolutely first-rate trap shot, was telling me this story. He was coming home from a big shoot when it started to rain; an oncoming car forced Dave to slam on his brakes and that threw him into a terrific skid. Dave's car spun around, demolished a car parked by the side of the road, smashed an outdoor phone booth and finally came to rest upside down on another car in a parking lot. Dave luckily came through all this with only a broken nose, four cracked ribs and his body completely covered with bruises. I asked him about his insurance and he sadly shook his head. "What's this going to cost you Dave," I questioned.

"Well, so far," he replied, "it's easily three birds out of every fifty."

EVENING SONGS

It's ALMOST dusk (what a lovely, soft word *dusk* is) and from the edge of the garden, by the bittersweet vines, some quail are calling. There are plenty of men who would offer to fight me if I suggested that there might just be a sound more thrilling than a fine hound in full blown cry, and I literally learned to walk holding on to the tail of a sweet voiced redbone named Queenie whom I dearly loved. But the unassuming mellowness of "bob white" does something different to me. A Canada honker black against the moon raises the hair on the back of my neck with his ancient music . . . and a wild gobbler can render anything else meaningless when you are waiting at sun-up in a forest of beeches. Call the turkey and the goose majestic when they sing and you don't really say enough. But let's not get lost in greatness all the time.

A quail call is a melody from a little gentleman. It doesn't boom out across the fields and hold you up tight in mid-step with awe; but you're no kin of mine if "bob white" doesn't bring a warmth and a feeling of rightness that pleasures you right up to the handle.

It's a little song from a little guy. Part of the harmony of a summer's evening . . . the presumptuous thumb-sized tree toad pretending to be some woodland giant, booms a bass note to hush up the screeching of locusts, and I have to smile at him. But when my garden covey's boss started to summon the women folk, I'd like more than anything else to find some way to say "Thank you." The horrors that exist in reality are, for too few moments, now pushed away by the fragile, lingering, delicate notes of "bob white." A few fastidious notes that leave the evening fresh and clean and sweet.

To the warrior, the long lingering thread-like brass of Taps can justify his day. But I'm humble in what music I require now. If the last sounds I ever heard were just "bob white . . . bob white" from the corner of my garden, by the bittersweet vines, it would indeed be quite enough.

DENTISTS

My good friend, Willis Paine, sent me a package that contained a book. When I opened it, the book carried the title *All I Know About Shooting*. And beneath the title was my name as author. Inside, the pages were all blank. But Bill is a dentist and since it's common knowledge that the whirring of the high-speed drill does strange things to their brains, we have to give dentists a little liberty in what they consider to be funny.

Now we all know that most dentists quickly attain the financial status of an Indian Raja and live forever amidst splendors.

But life isn't always what it seems. The money isn't always greener in the other fellow's job. Bill, like so many dentists, is a crack field shot. But his inability to hit trap and skeet targets is really funny. (Much funnier, really, than a book filled with blank pages!) As much as I coached him, Bill absolutely failed to improve. Fortunes were dangled before gunsmiths in the vain hope that an alteration in a stock or the change of a rib could solve the mystery.

His wardrobes of cashmere and silk shooting jackets were completely retailored lest the least impedance in his mounting and swinging of the shotgun should occur. Nothing worked. Then it finally dawned on me. Everytime a dentist says "PULL"—or even hears it he instinctively closes his eyes to avoid the anguish on his patient's face. This reflex is irreversible and accounts for the fact that to the best of my knowledge the longest run of targets by any dental surgeon has never exceeded four or five.

WISH BOOKS

FALL DOESN'T officially begin on my calendar until the postman starts stuffing my peeling red mailbox with the long-awaited catalogs from *Gokey's, L. L. Bean, Orvis, Herter's, Eddie Bauer,* and Bob Allen's *Gunclub Sportswear,* to mention just a few of my favorites. In my opinion, some of the best outdoor writing lies right there, in the rugged descriptive prose that captions the famous Bean boot or the man-to-man sentences that tell you how and why a particular down-filled parka will keep you unfrozen and comfortable in temperatures from 50 degrees above zero to 60 degrees below.

From one of George Herter's great works, his famous *Bull Cook Book,* I've learned that the proper way to make a great martini is to add a couple of drops of vinegar instead of the traditional vermouth. Bob Allen's advice to the trapshooter is worth reading twice and I can, with some considerable stretch of my imagination, believe that by trusting to the sartorial wisdom of Eddie Bauer, my appearance in the field will be uplifted to the point where I won't have to sneak in the back door of diners and will no longer frighten women and children.

I began wondering aloud how all these companies could afford to send out such expensive literature to so many guys . . . after all, there must be a limit to how many new pairs of boots and shooting jackets and red bandannas and suspenders and knife hones and insulated caps and so on that the outdoor fraternity can lose, wear out, or outgrow. My wife, as usual, overheard all this and responded by quietly ticking off the supplies of brush pants, suspenders, hip boots and the like that *I* have—in the attic, in the closet, in the garage, in the cellar, and further mentioned that if I could possibly think of any excuse to burden our dwindling storage space further she'd like to have equal time for a rebuttal. But she knows and I know and all the catalog people know that all they have to do is improve slightly on some perfectly satisfactory item that I already own and I'm back in the market—by air mail.

Not a little of the lure as far as I'm concerned is the thrill of getting a package in the mail. I wonder if people who grew up in the city areas feel the same way? Do you country boys remember the nights when everybody gathered around the kitchen table to leaf through the catalog from Sears? And how you always raced to get to the mailbox first, weeks before you could reasonably expect anything to have arrived?

I can't remember clearly what all the fascination was about. Do you? After all, you remembered exactly what was ordered, so what was the surprise? Seeing your name on the shipping label with a grown-up "Mr." in front of it . . . or perhaps it's as simple as just being *someone*, living *somewhere* and knowing that from far away there was someone else who knew that you existed there and had worn out or outgrown the three blue work shirts your mother had ordered last year and it was time for some new ones. Or the childish belief that someone is as glad to send you something as you are glad to get it. Whatever . . . as long as we're eager to get to the mailbox and pick up something sent to us from far away and still get that feeling of excitement of something new, there's enough farm boy left in us to see us through another new fall as if it were the first one ever and us going out again with our very first gun.

PUPPIES? YES!

I DON'T know how you are when it comes to temptation, but I'm a sucker. Or perhaps a better word would be "hardhead." The minute somebody tells me I can't do something . . . or shouldn't, my lips tighten, my common sense takes wing and I put my wrong foot forward—in a hurry. The point of all this is that a friend of mine has just offered me a pointer puppy. A very good-blooded pointer puppy. A very cute, liver and white, stove-lid footed, dreamy-eyed, tail-wagging, face-licking pointer puppy.

The guy who wrote "hope springs eternal in the human breast . . ." must have had an addiction like mine for puppies. And have I had puppies! And have I had hope! My first pup, when I was a grown-up, should-know-better gunner, was an absolutely gorgeous orange belton English setter called Jag. A silky haired siren that really worshipped the ground I planned to hunt over— especially if it had a couple of deer she could course for the rest of the day.

The next pup was a beady-eyed setter with far better papers than I'll ever sport, descended from royalty after royalty starting with a famous liver and white dog named Nugym. Little Ben was just too much pup that quickly became too much dog. Too smart, too fast, and absolutely convinced that he could fly. In fact he *did* catch a couple of quail on the flush . . . just about the only quail I ever brought back from an outing with him. I tried everything with Little Ben to keep him in some sort of contact with me. Starting with long running check cords of slippery nylon and ending with the symbolic effort of having him drag around three feet of enormous log chain, but Ben won out. He was a sensational bird finder and no one got a shot in the area he hunted in unless it was by chance, but, boy! Did we see birds in the air! They were small because we saw them from a great distance, but did we see birds!

I suppose a lot of it was my fault: maybe most of it. What Little Ben lived for was to see them fly. All I ended up being was transportation via station wagon, some scratching behind the ears and a source of food. Ben's companion was the wind; his goal, the far side of wherever he was. And I would end up alone scuffling along through the briars and hedgerows eking out a chancey walk up shot here and a shot there knowing full well that wherever Ben was, was where the action was . . . and that was a long, long way away.

So here I am. A two-time loser with pointing dogs. (My Labradors are another story.) And on the verge of losing my heart and patience and probably my lungs and wind to another puppy. But I can imagine that yet-to-come pup in a month or so pointing the robins on the lawn, chasing the butterflies and chewing holes in my socks. And I can imagine next fall—that mythical next fall— and the first solid, sure, know-what-I'm-about points. The rock steadiness, the easy handling to whistle, the soft retrieve, the pat on the head, the shared sandwich, the game coat lightly heavy with birds. The bragging . . .

That is exactly what I always see when I look into a pup's eyes and he looks into mine, but I guess he sees something different. A lot different. However I've got to have another pointing dog. The question before the court is not really why, but how. Do we swallow the dream again and get the young fellow and hope and work? Do we start looking for the three-year-old dog that's finished? Let's leave it for now with the fact that I'm tempted, and you can guess which way, I only hope my sock supply can stand it.

THE FIRST GUN

WHEN IN those somber moments before the fire alone . . . reflecting on the private splendor you've enjoyed behind the dogs that day; you stop and think about the old orchards; the few remaining chimney stones in some all-but-abandoned field that once was someone's home. I try to imagine a young man, a young bride and their dreams of a small and independent farm. A kitchen garden, a cow for milk, a hog or two . . . and now all that's left of the lady's touch is a rose or so, gone wild by the stones that mark the well; of the man's hard work remains just the outlines of the dream. Some stumps where some other field was planned, a tattered shed and some winter wood laid by that's gone to rot.

In the younger days of this land of ours, independence, nine times out of ten, meant a new frontier. Something just wrested from the wilderness, a place to be off by yourself. Well, today our frontiers are few—except those we take in little journeys, day by day. A bird cover. A deer stand. A bit of rock where the broadbills pass. And hopefully it has a "secret" feel about it. It's a place we find ourselves coming back to, time after treasured time. For birds, or deer perhaps, but more than likely just because we love the quiet of the place or the music of the nearby brook.

And that's kind of a long way around to tell you why my two small girls own guns. Not just guns of mine for them to use. But *theirs.* Now my girls are small, right now, by far too small to shoot, but not too small to understand that their own gun is some kind of key to the lost frontier, the secret place.

I believe that they will, as you have and I have, follow the guns, follow the dogs, to find some place that's been passed by by time.

I believe as strongly as I believe in anything in this world that having their own guns will make them better women. It will admit them to a society that I believe is real and true and honest.

A man today can't leave too much behind in terms of worldly goods. His children and their children have to get by as best they can. So I chose to leave an attitude about our woods and fields and swamps and ponds and frost and snow and nor'east squalls.

As long as there is such a thing as a wild goose I leave them the meaning of *freedom.* As long as there is such a thing as a cock pheasant I leave them the meaning of *beauty.* As long as there is such a thing as a hunting dog I leave them the meaning of *loyalty.* As long as there is such a thing as a man's own gun and a place to walk free with it I leave them the feeling of *responsibility.* This is part of what I believe I have given them when I have given them their first gun.

WHY

Once in a great while, when my wife shames me into it, we have a little party at the house. Invariably some meddling woman will notice the all-too-few woodcock shooting prints I have hanging on the wall or the all-too-few decoys in my sketchy collection. "You shoot *birds?* How *can* you?" And then I try to explain to her the difference between the swing-through method, the pointing-out method and maintained lead. If that doesn't confuse her out of any further remarks, she can be counted on to say "Oh I don't mean that. I mean how *could* you? The defenseless little things . . ." Mentioning the fact that she is wearing a leopard skin coat that was probably poached by some African with a poisoned arrow, has absolutely no relation to the conversation. Save your breath. *Birds* are different.

It's of no help either to try to explain the ecology of so much land—so many birds. It does no good to explain about nature's law of the survival of the fittest; or that she's just knocked back second helpings on Pheasant Fricassee; or to point out that without the restraining laws of nature and predation etc., etc., she'd be up to her sweet derrière in bobwhite quail or wild turkey.

What she wants to know—or have you admit, is that you are one hell of a killer, teeming with blood lust, who comes home from a few hours in a meadow or marsh with enough stiff game slung over your bloody shoulder to pull the rivets on your truss.

This, for some reason *I* don't understand, *she* understands and will accept as a perfectly valid reason. A friend of mine who makes his living, more or less, by working, more or less, for a gun company, is by nature a big game hunter. His answer as to why his house is decorated from cellar to attic with heads of antelope, impala and the outer garments of lion and leopard and zebra, is guaranteed to stop the nonsense. He merely smiles a very mysterious smile that I'm sure he's practiced over African campfires, and says "Oh, I guess I just like to hear the thud of bullets smack against some solid flesh."

But what happens when you ask yourself the very same question? Some excellent recent anthropology, notably Robert Ardrey's fine book *African Genesis,* claims that man owes his evolution to the fact that he learned how to kill. Ardrey has satisfactory evidence that man's first tools were killing instruments.

Maybe we kill just to keep our hand in, in case the job folds and we lose the mortgage and end up back in the father-in-law's cave.

The non-hunter doesn't understand why you and I can go out and swamp it all day long, not popping a cap or cutting a feather and be delighted, if not satisfied, with a nothing-to-nothing tie.

I guess I don't really believe that hunting is a *sport.* I tend to agree with Hemingway who said something to the effect that only mountain climbing, bull fighting and automobile racing were sports and that everything else was a game.

To me sport entails some grave element of risk. And hunting so rarely involves danger—not counting stupidity—that it doesn't qualify.

So let's say that hunting is neither a game nor sport. Trap and skeet are games and delightful, but hunting is a thing apart. It requires some involvement.

A lot of deep thinkers claim that hunting is largely a sexual thing. I won't or can't argue that. I tend pretty much to agree, but hunting has more than sexual undertones.

I think each of us understands it in his own way. You hunt for your reasons and I hunt for mine. And each of us is satisfied in his own way.

I think I hunt because I'm afraid of death and shooting is to me a very deep and complex way of understanding it and making me less afraid or more reconciled to my inevitable end.

I think I hunt because I envy wildlife and by having this control over their life is to share in it.

And I think I hunt because I have been hunted.

I know I hunt without regret, without apology and without the ability to really know why. Let's say I get a sense of satisfaction out of it that stretches back to the beginning of man's mind. I hunt because I am a man.

We are still young animals ourselves. Chronologically speaking we are only hours old compared to the birds, the fishes, and the bug that lays us out with flu.

We hunters share some ancestor wrapped in stinking robes of skin who would greatly envy us our three dram load of 8s as he stares at the polished shin bone of an antelope he holds cocked and balanced in his hand.

As the dog has the ancestral wolf, we have an ancestral killer too, tucked away, and not too deep, inside.

THE WOOD DUCK INVASION

THE OTHER morning we were sitting around the table at breakfast when we heard a soft whispering of wings coming from the study. Since the only birds normally encountered in my study are either wood, painted or stuffed, I rose to investigate. In the middle of the fireplace, perched saucily on top of the ashes, sat a female wood duck. I must have frightened her as I opened the door leading to the outside, for she flew out of the fireplace, landed on top of the book case and happily snuggled herself against a couple of decoys I have up there. Convinced that common sense would take hold and the open door would lure her out, the family and I left for the afternoon.

When we returned the house was a mess. There were duck feathers and spilled jars all over the kitchen. There were duck feathers upstairs. The only thing we couldn't find was the damned duck. (Do you know many places in *your* house where a small duck can hide?) I don't know if you've ever gone to bed with the firm knowledge that there is a silly hen wood duck just down the hall, for all practical purposes. Nor do I know how you'd react to a duck flying around the room at 3 A.M. I react badly. Very badly.

Luck was with me. I had to leave the house early and could lay the burden of the search on my wife and kids. My two Labrador retrievers, of course, showed not the slightest interest in all the goings-on. If I want them to retrieve a duck I have to shoot it first; this is the result of early lessons when I raised mallards. If I wanted to have a duck living in the house that was my business.

Later that day my wife called me at the office. The duck had been found, unharmed. Where was it? Just where you would be if you were a hen wood duck. Swimming around down in the dark corner of the cellar where the sump-pump lives in a 3-foot pond.

Now I feel kind of sorry for her. What's she going to tell her husband about where she spent the night? Like most women she probably had been carping about the tree they'd been nesting in and saw a far more splendid home nearby that turned out to be my chimney top. And, once in the room below, what was the first thing she saw. A dozen decoys! Plenty of extra room for another family . . . water in a nice dark room nearby. Perfect! Her mate will be reluctant to believe all this—at first. But the female of any species is a very powerful persuader indeed. And I fully expect before too long to hear a fluttering again in my fireplace and find not one wood duck sitting happily in the ashes staring up at the decoys—but two. And one will be telling the other "I told you so!"

OPTIMISM

I AM a born optimist—at least in April. The fact that I'm not always a clear thinker fades in memory from one year to the next. Every year I take the snow plow off the tractor one storm too soon.

This old optimist is going to build a shooter. That's right, build a shooter. Here's how it's done. You start with a boy somewhere in the neighborhood of twelve. You season him a little at first by letting him run the hundred yards and put up the rifle targets. Then you whip out some interesting looking piece of machinery. I think my .264 Winchester Magnum model 70 with an 8 X variable ought to perk him up. It's impressive looking and has a big bang akin to what the hammers of hell ought to sound like. I'll throw the scope off a bit and let him work through a box of shells putting it back where it was. That's a fine start for a boy. He's had a full sense of accomplishment. He's got the rifle shooting absolutely plumb and a sore shoulder to prove it. It may be just my theory, but I believe that a gun with a little bite in it is more fun to mess with than one that hasn't.

I'll let him go for about a week or so, thinking he's one hell of a shot and a fine fellow and start stage two. There's a little 28-gauge Daly over-and-under skeet gun and a hand trap to be reckoned with. I'll guarantee that this will prune the ego just a little bit more. Boys, like young trees, grow a little stronger with pruning. Stage three is working with the dogs. I've a pair of inexhaustible Labrador retrievers that need a "bird boy" just like him to help out with the training dummies. There's nothing quite like working with a dog to teach a boy a little loving patience and respect for the work that goes into becoming some sort of well rounded gunner. Now in a month or two I'll have something good started. A young man that knows nobody can hit everything he shoots at, a young man that knows that a good dog is as much a part of proper gunning as shells, and a fellow that ought to know by now that you brag about your shooting and your dog after the day is done—not before. I'll get him to some of the "big time" shoots and let him see what a first class retriever can do in a sanctioned trial. I want him to see the *best*.

What does it do to a man to see the best? To watch a Spirit Lake Duke take command of a field trial . . . or a Dan Orlich win everything that isn't nailed down? I hope it makes him an optimist. I hope it makes every tomorrow something that tingles him. I hope he sees every pup he'll ever own as a potential Duke . . . and every boy *he* builds as another Orlich. I'll even bet that some of his optimism will rub off on me when my supply starts running low. That may be all I'll need to get *my* 100 straight!

BRUSH PILES

WINTER IS a pretty sloppy housekeeper; as long as things are swept under the rug the place looks fine. But the time has come to do the cleaning up. It's not bad work compared to some. You get a fine sense of accomplishment building a brush pile. And a good brush pile, built just right (the care that used to go in learning how to stack a load of hay just right comes fresh to mind) to burn but not too quick or hot so you can't get close enough to tend it properly. A man I used to work with years ago would take a brush pile I'd build completely down and do it over according to the size and type of wood and when *he* was finished burning brush there'd be just a handful of ashes and no more.

I'm not that good or careful but I feel a sense of something good and old and honest when I heave to and make a pile of brush that I could point out to him with pride.

He was pretty fussy about the damndest things outdoors. His house, if you could call it that, would have had a little trouble with the board of health; but the backyard garden was a source of joy. His wood pile, hand cut by axe and bucksaw, was mathematical. Each hand split log was nested with its brother to form a wall so solid that the pile told *you* which logs to take and where they ought to come from.

He was a winter trapper too and I guess that's where plenty of the sense of order had its roots. He could look at a mink set a damned sight more suspiciously than any mink. And the sets I made were generally so full of faults he'd start to point them out as much as thirty yards away.

As I said, he had a sense of order. A feeling about the *rightness* of the thing. And luckily he took some interest in my stumbling love and understanding for the things he felt so strong about.

When the geese came back in some other May and rested for a day or two on our little lake nearby he'd tell me what they did in darkness—because he'd have stayed up all the night—just watching. He felt he ought to know.

The townsfolk used to call him "touched." He was; but not the way they meant. He didn't observe the world he lived from; he was part of it. They laughed behind his back but when someone needed honey it was Old John they came to ask about which hollow tree would have the dark brown wild combs.

I don't know what I'd say today about a man who took my boy of twelve and taught him how to fish, and stalk, and row a boat, and set a Blake and Lamb fox trap that would lure a fox, and I must admit he taught me how to poach and spear and smoke a nickel corncob pipe (with a slim pinch of fresh ground coffee mixed in to smooth out the edges).

He shot ducks over live callers when it was safe, but hardly legal, but only two or three to eat himself. And when he wanted fish he got them. Trotlines, spears or fykes were all the same to him. I'm sure the fish cared less than the game warden. The law can state the way of death but that doesn't make it any different to the dying.

Well, all that era's over. I don't poach—or haven't anyway for over 35 years. And I probably wouldn't do it right if I ever had the urge. Although I still have the fish fyke he made and gave me.

I've lost the knack of lots of things he insisted be done with a fine edge. And I'm a little bit ashamed of how too seldom in these times Old John comes back in memory to set right.

I'll build a good brush pile though this May, although nobody gives two hoots or even knows. It's funny how some things come back . . . worthless skills today . . . and lend a sense of pleasure to the meanest chores.

Maybe that's the answer. Maybe Old John took his dignity where he found it and although it wasn't much by most men's standards *he* would know that what he did was right—and more important cared about the least of outdoor jobs, to where they lent his life some inner purpose, no matter how the others felt who thought it weird to see him take such care in chores like stacking wood.

I don't make my living building perfect brush piles, but at least I care enough about such work to do it right.

There's a flight of geese that've come to spend the night in that big bend up the brook where the old willow slants the stream. And there's a twelve-year-old boy inside me that wants to creep up after dark and watch. I'll put a pinch of coffee in my pipe and sneak up later on and sit and listen. And I think I'll have company.

FRIENDS?

THERE COMES a time in every man's situation when he has to try to lie a little to his children to protect them from certain ugly sides of life until they are old enough to understand. For example, at this time of the year when I'm getting my stuff together to go out and have a few friendly rounds of skeet or trap or shoot a few patterns testing out a new reload I've concocted that mixes 8s with 9s, one of my little girls will ask "Why isn't Mr. Zern or Mr. Rikhoff going with you?"

I simply say that my friends Mr. Zern and Mr. Rikhoff have horrible hangovers and couldn't stand the noise . . . but the truth is that these otherwise good family men are "fishing." I once tried to explain to Patty, my seven-year old, what "fishing" was. I explained that Mr. Zern would put worms on a hook, that the hook was tied to a pole of wood with a piece of string and Mr. Zern or Mr. Rikhoff would then dangle this in front of a small trout or bass in an effort to catch him. I instantly realized my mistake when Patty, who has been reading the Waterfowl Regulations, along with wholesome stories from Churchill's "Game Shooting" and Greener's "The Gun and Its Development" instantly saw the thing clearly and burst into tears. I asked her what was the matter and she said sobbing "But Daddy, that's against the law." I asked her what law and she said Section so-and-so paragraph so-and-so.

I hurriedly looked it up and found that she was referring to the Federal laws against baiting. I tried to explain to her that it *did* seem like that but it really wasn't. And to further clear her mind I went out and got some hair bass bugs Jim Rikhoff had forgotten the night he was helping me test the specific gravity of some apple cider (the same night he drove all the way home with the emergency brake on and had to have the drums freed with a welding torch). I told Patty that certain men thought that if instead of using real bait, they used what they called artificials, as hair bugs certainly are, that this is the epitome of being sporting. She got the idea right away, although not at all pleased that the men she had admired for their ability to make light of her fathers whiskey and endure the rigors of pre-dawn goose pits and blistering August afternoons at Vandalia, Ohio, had this character flaw. So a little depressed at my lack of success at shielding her from these ugly facts of life, I watched her disappear into her playroom. A few hours later she came running into my study where I was busily putting a little Linseed on a few scratches in my Krieghoff stock.

"Daddy, we're rich, we're rich!" she shouted. And opening a cigar box she showed me what she'd been working on. In the box were some beech nuts, and some corn kernels, perfectly made of colored modeling clay and even a long roll of serrated earth-colored clay that made a fairly good imitation of an earthworm. I asked her what she thought she had. She said that if we made artificial corn, artificial beech nuts and fake worms, why couldn't we attract ducks, grouse and woodcock. That really wouldn't be baiting, it would be using artificials, and we could go into business and make bushels of money, which she thought, having listened to my wife's frequent discussions on the subject, we sorely needed. I explained to her that it wasn't the sort of thing a real bird shooter would stoop to doing, legality notwithstanding. I also pointed out that she had once seen Mr. Rikhoff drink a rum cola and so he was not to be trusted with an idea like plastic corn and that we would just forget it. But somehow the picture of Jim Rikhoff and Ed Zern holding up a brace of Pintails and saying how they "took them over half a peck of hand-made plastic Golden Bantam" sticks gloomily in my mind. Will the Federal authorities please advise?

THE HIGH SIERRAS

I WAS in the big country one winter watching the peaks of the high Sierras fill with snow. On my left were the ancient White Mountains. And etched across these sagebrush hills were the remnant paths of wagon tracks that seemed to come from nowhere and go nowhere. But I can see the men . . . trudging dustily alongside a mule, their eyes fastened on the next peak. I don't believe that in this country you look too close to where you are . . . it's next peak country . . . and the next peak . . . and then perhaps just one more.

This is the land of the visionary. The miner or farmer knee-deep in dust with visions of lush green pasture obscuring the chaparral and sage and tumbleweed, or the dreams of strikes of Eldorado or The Silver Queen cushioning the steady hammering of the pick in his hard-rock shaft.

Now, a man hunting birds is on a somewhat different scale of survival or adventure. But it wasn't too long until I began to feel some stirring in the blood to see what "the bear could see on the other side of the mountain." And I could see what lured us on 100 years ago. The thrill of the chase. See where the mule goes. Follow the ox. Or just plain go on alone.

So opens a new discovery to me as to another reason why we like to hunt. Perhaps it's just to follow the buck or the bird . . .

to see where he will go if he knows we're behind him. Of course we don't . . . or at least not very far. Except in our minds . . . where there is always just one more meadow beyond . . . one more stand of trees . . . one more mountain to offer us an unseen side. The magic of something that we've never seen before.

BE PREPARED

ROBERT BENCHLEY once remarked that the two most practical things he learned in four years at Harvard were that if you put one paper bag inside another you could carry draught beer and that if you turned your sock inside out, the hole would show up in a different place.

I'm in love with "tips." A few paragraphs entitled "101 Ways to Save Your Life with Aluminum Foil" instantly gets my undivided attention. Of course, when Nature has me by the throat in some forgotten bog 1000 miles from nowhere, the nearest source of foil will be some suburban A&P. I know how to start a roaring fire using wet wood with a candle that you've wisely stashed away, unfortunately in the coat you left at home, for just this emergency.

When I was a lot younger, perils were more real. I always carried some sort of savage beast or catastrophe around in my imagination—just in case . . . and I can vividly remember constantly praying for some sort of disaster to befall me so I could pit my wits against the forest primeval. It got so bad I wouldn't go out to feed the chickens without my Marble's waterproof match case.

I wanted to get lost so bad I can still taste it . . . and then when they found me, miraculously still alive after weeks alone, I would be warm and dry in a well-run camp. A haunch of venison would be turning on a spit and I would greet them with a look of complete mastery and unconcern on my face. I would have made buckets out of birch bark and my thick, soft bed of a fragrant nest of hemlock boughs. My larder would be stocked because I always carried a little roll of wire to make emergency snares.

If I was a half-mile from home, my little knapsack would have revealed spare dry socks. Extra mittens. Rope. A folding saw. Assorted nails. The stub of candle. A flashlight. Water purifying tablets. A folding cup. Bandages. Iodine. When the white picket gate shut behind me . . . I was always perfectly ready to take the short walk that would have brought me to the most magic of places. A name still comes to mind accompanied by the howl of frigid winds and the snarl of wolves against a background of blizzard snows . . . the mecca of ten-year-old pasture-trappers: *Hudson's Bay!*

But how we change! That same farm boy who literally slept with a half-axe was known, not long ago, to arrive at a trap shoot with his 16-gauge quail gun. But if we ever get lost together— you're in luck. I've got all the knowhow you will ever need. Provided, of course, you didn't forget the candle, the fish line, and the aluminum foil.

HEXES AND CHARMS

AFTER A recent trapshooting weekend was over I was all too well aware that about the only thing the winner and I had in common was hat size. On the way home I began mulling over all the thousands of tips and bits of advice I'd been subjected to and—to be honest—sought out avidly; I began mulling them over in my mind like a monk with his beads, trying vainly to hit some magic combination of ingredients that would turn my 1⅛ ounce of lead into gold—or if not gold, at least some kind of trophy. Any more fooling around with my trap gun was out. Lew Waltersdorf, a gunsmith and good and great friend, who has tinkered with my stock and triggers to the point of exhaustion, hinted that there was nothing more that he, or any other gunsmith, could do for me now. If the last refuge of the scoundrel is patriotism, then the last refuge of this shooter is the gunshop and that door has been closed.

The pitch and drop and length of pull have been altered and whittled so often that the stock is but a shabby sculpture of my own inadequacies.

After I had catalogued all the advice and honestly admitted that very little of it had done me any good, I got to thinking about the oddball things we all do in an effort to recapture *the day* when everything went right for us and/or everything went wrong for everyone else.

Some of the more useless idiocies I've been through are these: Buying a new trap jacket. (I won't tell *anyone* how many I have!) Getting a new hat to wear. (Same answer as above.) Putting chalk on the rib. (Some of the world's best shooters do this when they shoot live pigeon matches. I don't know why.)

Using a tiny front bead sight to create the optical illusion of longer barrels. (The next week a friend told me, after he'd run a hundred straight, that the reason was because he just put on an absolutely tremendous front sight—said it kept him from shooting over the straightaways. . . .)

One fact, however, is evident: shooting is like religion; it involves an attitude of faith. If you believe that this-or-that is a boon to your score, it will behoove you to trust that you are right. A Pennsylvania-Dutchman friend of mine has a hex sign on the stock of his trap gun and I can swear to its effectiveness. A while back he was high gun in a doubles event and I was the only shooter who could possibly beat him. His wife and my wife sat down on the bench with him to watch me shoot the last few pair. He sat there quietly rubbing the hex sign. One of the women asked him what he thought he was doing. "Putting the hex on Gene," he answered. And no sooner had he said that than I lost my last two birds—to finish second. "It always works," he remarked, as the women sat there open-mouthed while he cased his gun and put it back in the car.

I always feel better wearing a necktie when I shoot. One friend affects a ragged war-surplus tee shirt. And so it goes. Ancient sweaters, cowboy boots, baseball hat, lucky charms . . . what-have-you. Another friend says he puts a tenth of his winnings in the church poor box. (In which case they are not so poor—and if that would help me shoot as well as David, so would I!)

Next time you're out on the trap field and you see a guy wearing a necktie with a ragged tee-shirt and cowboy boots, who looks like he gives a tenth to the poor and has a hex sign on the butt of a shabby looking stock—say "hello." It's me again . . . looking for a substitute for skill.

MEMORIES OF MISSES PAST

It's sort of traditional at the end of the year to look back and take stock of what has happened during the last 12 months. One friend of mine keeps a diary. The regular kind, you might have seen one, for hunters and shooters. But a diary is pretty matter-of-fact. You sit around with a couple of your shooting buddies and one of them says, ". . . that was the day you had the double on green-wing teal . . ." Without a diary you can agree and return the compliment with something along the line of ". . . yes, that's right; I remember it well because it was just two weeks later *you* had a 94 at Grouse Ridge Gun Club . . ." and the evening is warm with the passing of such soft and sweet memories. But with a diary this never happens. The diary reveals that not only did you not double up on green-wing teal on that particular day (you did not one time double on anything, all year), you missed four easy incomers flaring out over the decoys and went home with two sea ducks. The diary would also reveal that George M. did not get a 94. The diary would read that as usual George M. was stopping his gun and lucked into an 87. The diary is to the shooter as the scale and the tape measure are to the fisherman—irrefutable proof that the judgment and memory of the outdoorsman improves, like a fine wine, with the passing of time. We're not in the business of facts and figures, anyway. Nobody's keeping score. Our end of the year inventory can have anything on the shelf we want. Two ruffed grouse can become eight or even ten or twelve. If you count the near misses, perhaps even a trifle more. The weather along the Chesapeake can get a lot colder and windier when you're sitting in front of a log fire a month later.

So instead of taking a long, hard look at the times gone by, let's take a softer dreamy one. Why not put your feet up on the good furniture and see what you'd like to have happened. This is nowhere near any form of lying—that's an art in itself. We're just looking at the truth from a variety of angles. Did Old Ben break into a covey of birds and flush them out of sight or do you suspect that he hit a running bunch of birds and did damn well to put them up so you could mark down the singles?

Did you really miss that huge old gander that came sailing in on set wings or did you just fire way behind him on purpose—sort of a parting salute? Did you really end up with only a 17 on your last round of trap or were you "working" with the gun to test the width of the pattern? Give it a little thought and you'll discover some nice smooth lines to shore up your story. I know one shooter who can barely hit the ground with his hat and after his usual two-shot miss he waves his gun barrel around very happily and says "Boy, that's what I'm out here for . . . just to see 'em fly!" He's carried on like this for so long that even *I'm* tempted to believe him. Trapshooters who have a long string of zeros will talk about how they're just polishing timing and rhythm. And one of the stupidest bird dogs I have ever seen is constantly praised by his owner for his "range."

So, look back and see what fits—from a different perspective. And next year start giving your Christmas presents early. Comment in admiration on some shooter's rhythm and timing. Slap your buddy on the back next time his dog busts every bird for a square mile and tell him how much you hate those close-working dogs that are always right there almost under your feet. And when we're together and it's one of those days when I'm a little bit off, it would be a kind thing for us to chat about sportsmanship and the bigger meaning of being out-of-doors.

BAD COOKS

I WAS innocently browsing through a pleasantly written and informative book on bird hunting by a pretty well-known outdoor writer, when I ran across a sentence that jarred me so strongly I almost spilled my glass of Jack Daniel's. The copyright laws being what they are, I can't quote it exactly but the meat of it is that if the author has been lucky enough to fill his limit on woodcock the next thing he does is look for someone with something like pheasant to exchange with. If that fails *he has his wife grind up the breasts* and throw them into some kind of meat pie casserole!

Can you imagine a man who does that? Why, he probably stirs champagne to get rid of the bubbles. Or fries black duck. My father is probably the worst cook in civilization. His coffee could be vastly improved by adding diesel fuel. His idea of cooking a venison steak is to fry it to the point where you could mistake it for a boot sole. He can't even make a decent sandwich; but even *he* remarked that a man who'd grind up woodcock breasts must be some sort of heathen.

How I feel about woodcock breasts, quickly sauteed in wine and brown butter, then salted and peppered, can be quickly surmised by the admission that one evening I ate nine birds by myself, washed down with a fine 1959 Saint Emilion. I would have eaten a few more but my wife had her greedy hands in the platter.

I will not, out of human decency, mention this writer's name
—lest he be hunted down and publicly ridiculed or worse—but I'm
sure you will all join me in wishing "The Curse of Ten Thousand
Flinches" on him whenever he's in woodcock cover. If any of you
have a recipe for boiled owl, I'll forward it. He'd probably lick his
lips.

THE ELEPHANT HUNT

It is not at all unusual for a man who loves to hunt to develop a fixation on a particular quarry. And it is not at all unusual for a man who has had the opportunity to hunt the world over to dwell on the taking of elephant.

Such was the aim of my friend; an aim heightened by the tantalizing experience of two previous safaris in Africa that had time and again discovered fresh elephant spoor only to have the beasts mysteriously disappear, as only elephant can, at the last possible moment.

After the last unsuccessful trip my friend's attitude toward the elephant changed. He began to believe that he had simply been outsmarted. Having once been a fine soldier he knew that one of the greatest mistakes in war is to underestimate the intelligence of your enemy. Now he began to apply this truth to the hunt. He began the rapid and thorough accumulation of an enormous amount of elephant lore. Everything there was to read, he read. He screened thousands of feet of film involving the African elephant. He made the acquaintance of anyone who was known to have hunted the animals. He even spent hours at the zoo staring at their corrugated leather hides, and asking probing questions of their keepers.

While I know that animals lack anything approaching a man's

ability to reason, I believe that a man under this sort of obsession can, in time, see himself simultaneously as both the hunter and the hunted. I believe that such a dream as my friend had—whatever his deep reasons—can become an obsession not unlike the fervor of Ahab to seek out Moby Dick, the great white whale.

Why does a man get so driven to take a particular animal? I don't know. Perhaps there is some atavistic urge that some people feel more strongly than others. Perhaps in our genes and chromosomes still exist the remnants of ancient tribal rites or cultism—the forerunners of modern religion—back to the days when there were groups who "worshipped" the lion, the leopard, the crocodile, and of course, the elephant. It may be all of this—and the common belief that still exists in parts of the world that by taking the life of a great animal you assume some of his courage and you extend the days of your life beyond their allotted span.

Perhaps this last answer makes the most sense, because the days of my friend's life were certainly numbered. In the 240 pounds he carried on his frame of six-foot-five were a few ounces of cancer.

At last the long-expected call from Nairobi came. The white hunter had found a great elephant, the trip had been arranged, the game sector had been reserved. Could he catch the next plane? The stage was set.

In spite of the terrible agony it cost him, my friend insisted that the basic safari be done on foot. From the first camp they began the walk that would come to last for nearly two long weeks. Nights were spent sleeping on the ground—brief stretches of calm between waves of pain. And, day after day, he carried alike his dream and the cruel worm inside him.

As the chase began to fall into a pattern, my friend began more and more to identify with the elephant they were following. The great oval footprints in the dust were now as familiar to him as the thrust of his own. The moves of the elephant were as his moves. He and the animal had become one being—linked together by a destiny that neither could avoid—or wanted to, it seemed.

Now with the elephant frequently in hearing ahead, there was no need to hurry. A day or two or three now made no difference. In effect the hunt was over—except the final act.

Ahead was a waterhole and my friend had correctly guessed that this was the place that the old elephant was looking for. So, by making a large circle ahead, he came to the oasis and hid himself and waited for the huge grey beast to meet him there.

"I wanted the hunt to go on forever," he told me later, "but I felt that to pursue him any longer would involve a cruelty I couldn't permit.

"It was almost dark at the waterhole and the silence was oppressive. Then suddenly I realized that the old man had been standing at the edge of the clearing and staring at me for a few minutes without my seeing him. There we were now peering at each other through squinty eyes as if we were old friends who hadn't seen each other for years and could think of nothing to say for the moment. He had only one tusk and my first thought was to try to imagine the monumental pain he must have felt when the other one was broken off. After about fifteen minutes of looking each other over I decided that I had kept him waiting long enough. I got to my feet, holding my rifle in my hand, a visitor in a friend's home who is ready to take his leave. The old man across the waterhole seemed to understand. He turned around, took a silent few steps and closed the door of the darkened forest behind him.

"We rested at the waterhole for a few days and then walked the long way back."

When he had finished telling me the story, my friend leaned forward in his chair, and tapped the glass doors of his guncase with the tip of the cane he was now forced to carry. "Perhaps," he said, "when all is said and done we come to learn that the greatest pleasure in owning a gun is discovering the great privilege of not using it."

GOOD WORDS

I'VE BEEN lucky enough to receive from my readers some fine evocative letters. Most of them are so well written and warm that I get to feeling like a pitcher in the late innings who's a bit shocked to find that the catcher is throwing the ball back a lot harder than he's getting it over the plate. I enjoy them all; each one is like making a new friend. I got one from a gentleman that contains a couple of sentences so singularly magnificent I'd like to share them: "I sure miss the old duck-hunting days and I often look back at them, but as I am 79 years old, was born in 1889. I thought I better write and tell you I still am left while I still am. Things are not the way they used to be."

I'd like to say that I answer all my mail, but that would be treading a little gingerly on the truth. Like most writers I'm lazy. And my editors would probably go further than that; they're constantly in some state or other of worry about my being perpetually late with my copy. Editors and writers enjoy the same relationship as dogs and fleas. But I won't say which is which.

FREE ADVICE

AFTER THE smoke and thunder had finally stopped at a recent trap shoot it was discovered that my name was among the winners. No one was more surprised than I was (no, that's not likely to be true at any shoot where I'm known . . .) when my name was called to come up and receive my prizes. I accepted them with no humility at all and mouthed the customary "Thank You . . ." But as I stood there I couldn't help but imagine how I *should* have accepted the trophies . . . the same way movie stars accept theirs—something like this:

"Thank you all very much, but a man doesn't win a thing like this by himself. It's the people *behind* me that really deserve the award. They're the ones who made it all possible. So I'd like to extend my heartfelt thanks and deepest gratitude to my great and good friends George Schielke and Lew Waltersdorf who have toiled ceaselessly over my shotguns in their supporting role as gunsmiths. My thanks to Abercrombie & Fitch who have so kindly furnished my wardrobe on shaky credit. And a word of appreciation to my many coaches: among them, Dick Baldwin of Remington, who told me I was standing too straight. Mr. Dave George who told me I was standing too bent over. Burt England who said I was shooting too fast. And Ralph Matragrano who said I was shooting too slow. Mr. David Crosby who reminded me that I shoot better with my head off the comb slightly and Mr. Geroge Martin who insisted that I glue my cheek to the stock. And all the other helpful friends who were constantly mindful that I was holding my gun too high or too low; that my feet were too far apart or too close together and that my stock was either too long or too short for me."

(At the end of my speech, while the room rocks with applause, a film of other credits is projected for the benefit of all . . . Mr. Hill's shooting coat by Bob Allen . . . glasses by Bud Decot . . . guns by Krieghoff . . . makeup by Vaseline . . . etc., etc. Overall Technical Management and Supervision by Mrs. Hill.)

THE PRIMROSE PATH

THERE ARE certain natural laws that we have all learned to live with that are as constant and valid as the fact of gravity. Laws like "if anything can possibly go wrong it will." "Nothing is impossible to the man who doesn't have to do it." Never do today what can be put off until tomorrow." "Things are never as bad as they seem . . . they're usually worse."

Now, what our language is sorely missing is some law to explain the phenomena that happen to the guy who likes to spend a little time out-of-doors. You likely know the pattern all too well. It starts in a variety of ways but buying a puppy is as common as any. Now, more than not, one of the first dogs you think of is an English setter—just because they're pretty. Then you discover as the dog is growing up that it is pointing the robins on the lawn. So you figure if the dog will point robins . . . why not take the next logical step and see if it will point quail or pheasants? Unhappily for you—it does.

The next step is borrowing a neighbor's gun and buying a license to take a shot or two to see if the dog can help you pick up a nice bird or so for Sunday dinner. Then it's hunting clothes. Memberships in a local gun club to practice your wing shooting. Then it's discovered that you need at least *three* guns: one for birds, one for skeet, one for trap. Then it's either a lot of expensive trips to find better bird hunting or an expensive membership in a shooting preserve. Now your dog is in heat and you start looking for a good male so you can have just one more dog. Or vice versa.

You now have at least three guns, an enormous wardrobe of gear, memberships in various gun clubs, shooting clubs, field trial and dog clubs. And you've traded in a perfectly good family sedan for a new station wagon. You start smoking a pipe. You discover that the pleasant smell around the fire in the lodge is only part woodsmoke—the other part is bourbon. You seem to get sick a lot in the fall so you can't show up at the office. You have started to shout DOWN! HUP! OVER! at your children and barely caught yourself in time to keep from telling your wife HEEL! Your good suit is always covered with dog hair and so is the house and the car. There are teeth marks in all the chair rungs and your good leather boots. Your expensive shrubbery is a horror and none of the words a preacher uses on Sunday could describe your lawn.

But not to mind. A man can have worse habits than three guns and some bird dogs—not more expensive or time consuming—but there are worse.

Pretty soon a friend of yours will stop over and start chucking your puppy behind those silken ears and begin asking your advice. Chances are you will start to speak with forked tongue as our Indian friends used to say. You will describe the dawn smell of the meadows with a soft persuasive voice . . . speak lightly of your acquired skill with a shotgun and dwell longingly on campfires and twilights as you top his glass with a fresh dash or two. You offer him your can of Brushsmoke to fill his pipe. By now he's too far swept away into some imagined October afternoon to notice that his suit is covered with dog hair and pipe ashes have scorched little holes in his tie.

You lend him your copy of Ray Holland's *Seven Grand Gun Dogs* and Burton Spiller's *Firelight* and send him off to sail by new stars.

It's just another one of nature's immutable laws that we are all bound by. Some might say that it's "Misery loves company." But we know better. It's really more like "God doesn't count the hours man spends afield with friends," or "The thing we build that lasts longest is memory." All we ever need to do to hear the sounds of geese is listen. All we ever need to do to see the point and the flush is to close our eyes.

WITNESSES

THERE'S AN old proverb that goes "A kiss without a moustache is like an egg without salt." And so it is with hunting stories—like eggs, they require salt. But some require less salt than others. Especially when you're surrounded by witnesses. Now, I don't know how many of you who are reading this have ever had witnesses to a spectacular feat afield, but the guy who wrote it has had damn few. Not that I've pulled off too many, to be honest about it, but I've just got the feeling that if and when something comes up my only support will be a Labrador retriever and she'll probably be looking the other way. One of the things I've always wanted to do is to pick off a tough incomer on quail and then catch the bird in my hand. I've especially wanted to do it since I saw Bob Stewart do it. Another friend had an absolutely pure triple rise on ruffed grouse and his old Remington did it three times and he stood there—alone among men—and with two witnesses, not counting Pepper, his pointer. You know where the nearest human would be if you or I had a triple on grouse? Four miles away drinking cider.

But, I'm not being fully honest. I *have* had witnesses—in fact, on days like these I *always* have witnesses. The day Jim and I missed about seven pheasants in a row over lovely old Belle in an open field. The day I missed three bucks at 60 yards standing together in a sumac patch. The day . . . well, I could go on, but lest you soil these pages with tears of compassion, best we forbear. However, as you know all too well, the sun don't shine on the same dog's posterior every day. But it shone on old Dick Wolter's pretty good the day he made an absolutely magnificent crossing shot in a thick patch of honeysuckle with the sun in his eyes. Only thing was that the ruffed grouse Dick thought he'd brought down in Olympic style turned out, on rather casual inspection, to be an old Rhode Island Red. Now none of Dick's four witnesses can remember their wedding anniversary or come within a fortnight of their wife's birthday . . . but if you want to see feats of total recall, just mention Rhode Island Red!

GOING BACK

ONE OF the most satisfying things about shooting is that over the years you build a storehouse of secret treasures. I mean all the places you have been where something happened. A brush pile that had a sunning buck sleeping behind it. The little cedar copse where you almost got a double on pheasant. The patch of Indian grass behind the tumble-down barn where Little Ben pointed a 20-bird covey. Just to go back to them now brings it all together again. You approach the places with the picture in your mind of that special yesterday . . . your step softens and you seem to hesitate—not sure whether or not it will happen again—yet too sure that it will not. And though it really never comes to life again, the magic of the time the air was filled with a flitting woodcock lingers on.

Not too long ago, I went back and walked along a long-remembered brook; a brook that I had carried in my mind since I was nine or ten. Memory pictured a deep-holed mysterious run of water, broad and swift, that brought back all the awe that stared through a youngster's eyes.

But the brook itself the other day was something else. A turgid piddling trickle that eased itself around the rocks with every evidence of strain and effort. The deep dark holes were vanished.

The cascades that I so vividly recalled were muted tumblings that fell softly onto mossy stones. Yet, as I stood the familiar things came back. A tree, a tent of stone slabs where I once set a trap for coon—all there still exactly as they had been, years and years ago. The *brook* was just the same as it had always been. Something had gone wrong with *me*. My need for magic had grown too big for such a brook to stir me now. So I would wait a while and see if that sleepy run of stream could carry off some years. And so it did. In a little while, the noises grew into the remembered waterfalls, the rocks strained again against the force of flow. The shadows deepened and the secret feeling tiptoed back. When everything was once again just right I left, but my old boots now erased the footsteps of the trapper, ten years old, who had walked before me on this self-same path.

WHY NOT?

MY PERSONAL philosophy in many areas has been the simplistic attitude of "why not?" Not only does this reflect a certain lack of serious thinking on my part, but it shows how lightly I regard future consequences. Ordering new guns, for example, shows that one forgets or ignores the fact that one will not have any more money to spend on guns in six months from now than one has in his pocket at the moment. One will, no doubt, have to go to the bank again and say he is building another new bathroom and acquire a home owner's loan. Another shameful experience (shameful is not exactly the right word as you will see) is coming downstairs on Saturday morning in your gunning clothes because you said "why not?" to some invitation and discovering the family all dressed up and waiting for you to take them to the zoo—because when they asked you about *that* you again said "why not?"

A man who is shortsighted enough to go around saying "why not?" like a parrot with the IQ of a clay target is also not the kind of guy who keeps any sort of engagement calendar. "Why not?" has resulted in my wife preparing a meal for eight when she expected three. And once in a while someone else has to drive me home, or put me up for the night, because they broke out the Virginia Gentleman or Jack Daniel's after dinner.

On the other, or positive, hand are the pleasures you can have when you toss yourself on the seas like a bottle to find out where you'll turn up next. You remember the story of the man who in his final breaths called in his family and said "I must apologize to you all. I suppose I haven't been the perfect father and husband. I shamefully admit that I spent as much of my life as I could with the guns and the dogs. I was rarely at home during the hunting seasons and I'll admit that I spent too much time at the gun club." He paused here to rest for a minute, then continued. "I've been a terrible father and I hope you all forgive me." He paused again and looked around. Then he closed his eyes and smiled and said in a half-whisper to himself, "and on the other hand . . . I *have* shot a helluva lot of birds."

AN EVENING WALK

IT'S BECOMING sort of a habit with me to take a short walk out in the meadow as the sun is setting so I can walk back home in the afterglow at the edge of the night. I guess it's as much to see to it that the pheasants are asleep and to wake up the owls as it is to taste and smell the change of air from light to dark. Aside from the pitching and stumbling over the black Labradors, which insist on walking between my legs, I find this an exercise in tranquillity second to none. Woodcock come dusking over my head from one hidden cover to another secret place to probe for worms. Eight mallards are nervously gossiping in the pond, and two young does, this year's twin fawns almost certainly, are staring at me in hopes that I'll turn invisible so they can go on nuzzling the leaves on the young willows I planted last April. I'm getting the feeling that I'm intruding on the peace and go along about my business, guided home by the star of light gleaming from the kitchen window.

A few steps ahead is the unseen outline of Tippy who has stopped in the sure knowledge that I will fall over her once more. Under the crabgrass lawn the moles are busily mining the roots of the peonies and serving each other bits of prize tulip bulbs. The ducks and muskrats are turning the pond into a gelid mass of mud and the owls are, no doubt, praying for the day when I start to raise chickens. My apples are so wormy that even the squirrels that live in the attic disdain them. I pass by the chance for a goodnight peek at the sheep, certain that they've discovered a hole in the fence. And certain too, now, that I have forgotten to get bourbon, I track my muddy feet across the newly washed kitchen floor. Shooed outside to take my boots off, I stand there quietly. A little cold and a little damp, I pause between the moles underneath and the owls overhead and realize that the true glory of man is in his role of the spectator. We cannot change the ultimate lives of the creatures we harbor in our world, but now and then by watching them we can gain some sense of what we are and just where we stand on the shelf . . . somewhere between the owls and the moles.

THE WAGER

I was hanging around the trap club the other Sunday debating whether or not to play the purse on the handicap, when a new squad number was called for the end of the 16-yard event. One of the guys, sort of talking to himself, as I guess we all do, in the vain hope that we'll listen to the guy we love best, said a little more out loud then he wanted to, "This time we're going to break a hundred straight!"

A friend of his happened to overhear this personal prayer and caught us all slightly embarrassed by shouting "Archie you couldn't break a hundred targets shooting straight into the carton they come in!" Let me assure you right here and now that the room fell dead silent—everyone was instantly intrigued with the idea as I was. Archie paused, reflected, smiled and as they say "a wager was struck."

The squad old Arch was in decided they would be delighted to wait to shoot. Everybody wanted to see the results of "shooting them on the nest," so to speak. A trap boy got a carton of clay targets, holding 135 as you undoubtedly know, opened them to make sure none were broken already, and then they paced off a rough 32 yards—about the distance a decent trap shot breaks his singles targets—put the box on the ground and came back to join what was now quite an appreciable crowd. Needless to say there

was some flurry of side betting. He slipped a three dram load of
7½s in the full choke barrel of his Winchester 101 trap gun and
taking very considerable care with his aim, fired. The carton was
seen to jump slightly; hit and hit solid. The trap boy went out
and carefully returned the goods. From the outside the box was
riddled.

Now, like practiced archeologists sifting the remains of a lost
pharaoh, the unbroken targets were lifted from the box and set
aside. How many do you think he got? Just 63!

RAISING PUPPIES

BY THE time this piece gets into print I'll be up to my well-chewed ankles in Labrador puppies. I'll have picked out a bitch for myself, already named "Trouble" by my daughters, and the training will be just under way. I like to take the whole passel of pups on long walks. They learn how to negotiate all sorts of problems this way and develop their curiosity. The shy pups grow bolder and the bold pups learn some common sense. If I was forced to name one single characteristic I look for in choosing a puppy—for any kind of gunning work—I'd have to say curiosity, or to put it another way, tempered boldness. You can see this kind of puppy think its way through a new situation, correcting his mistakes and learning at a steady pace as he grows wiser.

Training is essentially a process of getting *your* dog to do things *your* way. But first you should know what a dog is capable of—not necessarily just your dog—but dogs of that breed. And the best way to do this is to watch field trials. A lot of people say, with some justification, that field trials are artificial. But in reality field trials demand a lot more from a dog than day-to-day hunting. An All-Age Open Labrador trial will have a variety of tests that are far more difficult than you might ever encounter in duck shooting. But the purpose of the trial is to show the judges how good the dog is and ordinary "gun-dog" situations don't tax these fellows at all.

You've heard the same stuff about trap and skeet. A gunner will say "Okay, so he can shoot 100 straight here—but I'll do a lot better in the field." Well, don't bet your shell money on it. I've seen Dave Crosby, who has been a Great Eastern Skeet Champion, shoot for days in the field and never have to dirty the second barrel!

Next to seeing some field trials—or, better, in addition to seeing some—there are several good books on training, like R. A. Wolters' *Water Dog*. Two other excellent retriever training books are by Charley Morgan and James Lamb Free. I suggest you get them all. For pointing dogs, you should read *Gun Dog* by Wolters, *Bird Dog Training* by Henry P. Davis, *Wing and Shot* by Wehle. Another great book that's out of print, but well worth looking for, is *Training the Bird Dog* by Whitford.

One word of caution: take your time first and get to know your dog. Be sure of his basic temperament and guide yourself accordingly. Hard dogs can be worked one way and soft dogs another; in certain situations the bold dog becomes shy and the timid dog works like a tiger. Not everyone will agree with me but I'm a firm believer in a gun dog being a house dog too. Why? Simply that the more time you spend with your dog the more you will become a team—each learning more about the other and finding a deep understanding.

I freely admit that if I were without a dog I wouldn't hunt birds. And I'm not overly particular about the breed of dog. I like them all—pointers, setters, retrievers, spaniels—what have you. I've had good ones and bad of several kinds. Most of the bad ones were my fault and most of the good ones would have been good under any circumstances.

JENNIFER ASKS "WHY?"

MY LITTLE GIRL, Jennifer, and I were mussing around with one of the Labradors and, as more often than not, we found a tick lodged in the inside tip of her ear. Jennifer deftly removed it and ground it under her heel. "What is a tick?" she asked me.

I started to explain that a tick was an eight-legged insect something like a spider and that I thought they belonged to the same class, *Arachnida*, when she stopped my shallow wanderings and re-phrased the question, "I don't mean that, I mean *why* are ticks?" I said I didn't even know why there were dogs. Then, being in a silly mood, I proceeded with the ancient excuse for giving a straight an-swer by asking her if she had ever considered that maybe there are dogs so that ticks would have something to bite; and that the reason little girls have fathers is that otherwise little girls wouldn't have anybody to tease with their silly questions.

That seemed to settle the original question about the tick but somehow I got going on and on in the same ridiculous tangent. Maybe, I told her, we have wives that shriek at us so we'll get out of the house to go outside and hunt. And we hunt because we need an excuse to own a houseful of dogs. And we need a houseful of dogs to support the ticks. The outcome of this magnificent logic is that we have ticks, so we are forced to get married. Having satis-fied both Jennifer's sharp mind and my own circuitous one I sent her out to the herb garden to pick me some mint leaves. If she asked me why are there mint leaves I swore to myself that I would teach her to be the first five-year-old of my acquaintance who would know how to construct a suitable mint julep. If she asks me why there are mint juleps I will have a helluva good answer. I will point to her mother.

THE PERFECT GUN

THIS IS the season of trap and skeet tournaments. The time of the dreamer has come and the sound of "PULL" is heard o'er the land. And the dream for the trapshooter is, of course, the perfect gun. Not the perfect score, but the perfect gun. The trapshooter sees in his mind's eye a very special single barrel or superposed, according to his bent. It is perfectly choked for the shell he likes the very best. The stock is of such magnificent walnut that other men will gather for hours just to stare at the convolutions of the burl. The drop and length of pull are of such exquisite dimensions as to make mechanical measurements a sacrilege. The trigger release is accomplished by an imperceptible pressure of the forefinger at exactly the right time. It never creeps . . . it would never, never, double.

And of course the gun would be tastefully engraved. A single pigeon in gold set amidst a fine line arabesque . . . and the owners initials in Old English script would grace the trigger guard. It would have 30- or 32-inch barrels and the balance point would be so magic in its placement that the eight-pound weight would be as nothing.

Now suppose the average trapshooter did get his dream . . . actually owned the perfect gun. Would he sooner or later start mussing with the height of comb? Right. Would he fiddle with the weight? Absolutely. Would the gun end up with electricians tape

or great slabs of leather on the magnificent burl? Right again. I
would bet a case of 2 ¾ 8s against a handful of spent primers that
the average trapshooter (notice I mention no names . . .) knows
of three grades of gun. *Perfect. More Perfect* and *Somebody
Else's.* The trapshooter's version of hell would be to sit before the
everlasting fires showing off a perfect Purdey over-and-under that
never misses a target and Old Scratch absolutely forbidding the
shooter to even mess with the choke, fool with the trigger, or
jimmy around with the wood.

GETTING READY

ALONG ABOUT now when the first of the cooling evenings sends the
fog sliding thickly through the meadow—so heavy that I can barely
see the top of the split rail fence—I feel the urge to *get ready*. My
wood ducks are itchy to leave and now and then from somewhere
high a Canada goose reminds me to get moving. The odd woodcock has already been seen along the lane. The shaggy bark
hickory is shrugging off its summer green and I can start walking
across the lawn without feeling guilty that I'm not pushing the
mower. And when I can really forget that I forgot to take down
the storm windows last spring; it's time to get ready.

I guess everybody starts a little differently. In the back closet,
most with a few tooth marks from times when Tip or Ben or Judy
was a pup, and often with a touch of last year's mud, are the
boots.

I always want to use the English waterproofing method of
half filling each of the leather boots with warmed neatsfoot oil and
let them sit—but I never seem to have any neatsfoot oil handy. So I
do the next best thing. I light a little fire in the room where my
books are and let the boots get warm then give them a good
coating of waterproof paste. I'll read a little bit while that soaks in.
If I remember to buy them, I'll thread in a new set of laces; if not
I'll tie new knots in the old ones. I've got an old toothbrush to get

the gunk down in around the soles and worry the briar scratches the best I can. Some would say they look pretty down and out— but I know briars put character in a boot and I like that.

After the boots are done the next step is the hunting coats. With me hunting coats are always somewhat of a problem. The fact behind that is that I shift back and forth (for no really good reason) between a 12-gauge, a 16-gauge, and a 28-gauge. So, by the end of the year, each coat has an assortment of shells of various sizes. I originally started out, very logically, by having a 12-gauge coat, a 16-gauge coat, and a 28-gauge coat. But I got to grabbing the 16-gauge coat and the 12-gauge gun and have ended up rummaging around general stores trying to find something smaller than magnum fours (which is all they ever seem to carry) in order to have a pass or two at ruffed grouse. If you try to find 28-gauge shells in most of the back-water gas stations or groceries they just plain think you're bonkers. Anyway, I have to sort shells and point out the necessary mending to the Queen Bee. After the 12-gauge shells are restored to the 12-gauge coat and so on down the line, the brush pants are separated from the old red handkerchiefs wadded up in the hip pockets, the lost pocket knives are found and the nickels and dimes are swooped up by the girls for their banks, order is seen to be taking form. The britches are let out their annual inch in the seat and the annual question "Why don't you throw these old pants out?" is answered by the annual "I will, after I get one more season's wear."

This ritual over, borne patiently but disinterestedly by the dogs, the guns are seen to. Everything in the gun rack is shifted. The trap and skeet guns are moved to the end of the row and the three bird guns put back up front. The dog whistles are found and hung back on their pegs. The gunning glasses are cleaned and the folding cup washed. To the eye of a casual visitor I am now READY. And on the surface, all things in order, it would, indeed seem a neat and meticulous chap is ready to step under his cap and set out. Not yet. For it is only September—teasing us a little with soft fog and a cool evening.

For in the coming weeks the earnest work goes on. The long walks to slim the overfed dogs and the overfed feeder of dogs. The long walks delicious in the prospect of searching out a new or at least long-forgotten cover and reassurance that the natural order of things is in good shape for at least one more fall.

There has come a time in my life when the planting of the tree is at least as enjoyable as the picking of the fruit. We do not see the later chores of pruning. Nor the invasions of leaf borers nor the weight of ice too great for limbs to bear. Only when you plant an apple tree can you honestly imagine perfect apples.

When you prepare early for fall then, and only then, do you have fall perfect; fall without worms. The October seen in September is the October of the landscape artist. It is the October of a small boy, an eager hunting dog or a middle-aged bird hunter.

So, I think, it is with we who live to be outside. No day is ever separate from the tomorrow to come. If we miss now, we'll hit the next time out. That's why dogs bury bones—for tomorrow. If I buried a bone I'd probably forget where I did it. But as long as it's on my mind, I think I'll get up and sprinkle a few 28s in my 12-gauge coat and some 16s in my 28-gauge coat. No old dog can outsmart me when it comes to getting ready.

SWEET DREAMS

HAVE YOU ever noticed how empty a field looks just after the last
deer has jumped over the fence? Or how quiet the marsh becomes
when the rooster has flushed and flown leaving you nothing to
hear but the wind? Or how a pair of mallards hung between the
setting sun can make all of your worries seem insignificant and
powerless?

They don't tell bedtime stories to grown-ups to comfort us—
although I can think of a thousand nights when a story with a
happy ending would have brought a sweeter dream—so I use
things like these to ease a troubled sleep. There's a part of us inside
that will never grow up; our glass of cheer is always half full, never
half empty. Someday we'll find the perfect gun and perfect dog
and live happily ever after. Meanwhile the harsh dark hours of the
night are softened and made light by well-remembered memories
of pups and quail and unexpected deer and geese that arrived in
time to save a day we almost considered lost. I know that a woodcock I once saw years ago against the evening star has flown me
softly through evenings that I would have dreaded had I been
alone without him.

RAISING PUPPIES, PART II

I ONCE glibly mentioned that I was expecting some Labrador puppies. I further gave notice that I was a fairly strict dog man and that a rather tight regime of training was to be initiated shortly after weaning took place. I may even have been foolish enough to have bragged. In any event, I now offer a report.

When the puppies, two females and one male, were about six months old this is what they learned: if they throw themselves at the screen door hard enough, the screen will tear out and they can come into the house at will until I replace the screens (which I haven't yet). They have learned that if they get way back under the couch I can't reach them and that I will tire of calling them and I will go away and let them sleep. They have learned that it is easier to dig holes in soil that I have laboriously cultivated, so my flower beds, garden, and lawn are heart warming sights to anyone who ever served in the artillery. The heavy artillery. They have learned that if they chew up one of my sneakers I will give them the other one. They also know that I can't always tell them apart so it's a three-to-one chance to ignore being called—in their favor. They know that my daughters will allow them to sleep on the bed. That my wife will give them gourmet meals while I subsist on cereal and skimmed milk. If they require an afternoon snack their grandmother, Tippy, will take them up to the garden and knock down corn and husk it for them. If there was any corn left, which there isn't now, no one is husking it for me. They know that they can badger me into throwing tennis balls for them when I have work to do. They know it's a waste of effort to jump on me when I'm wearing work clothes and save this kind of play until I'm dressed up.

I'm presently amusing them by my efforts in building a kennel and run. They have eaten the larch trees I planted for shade and have run off with the hammer more times than you'd believe. Right now it's a race against time. Will I get it built soon enough to save the few things they haven't gotten into—or will the kennel be the only thing left standing amidst the ruins? Anyway, if I have to go on welfare because I've gone broke buying screen doors—they'll be sorry! The man who said "The only experience a man can't recover from is hanging," is wrong. He never tried to raise three Labrador puppies.

THE OLD SONGS

Sing me the old songs.

Tell me the stories of times gone by.

I want to spend an evening or so with you to hear about your
dogs.
   I want to see your guns.
   I want to read your favorite books.
   I want to warm my hands in front of your fire and try your pipe
   tobacco and taste your whisky.

I want to see the old brown pictures you've always saved.
   The pictures of the stern-faced men wearing hip boots and
   brown overalls with rusty wool caps pulled down over their
   eyes.
   The pictures of men who wore neckties and soft flannel shirts
   and breeches and leggings standing by braces of stiff-necked,
   rib-sprung pointers with the quail wagons behind them.

   I want to see yourself in a blue work shirt buttoned at the neck,
   with your kitchen haircut and your .22 and that big-eyed
   pup.

Do you remember all the names?
  Tell me them.
  Talk to me about the horses.
  Talk to me about the dogs.
  And the L. C. Smith, The Parker, the Baker, the Lefever and the
    Ansley H. Fox.

Tell me about the cold and the wind and the sea and the river and
    the kettle pond.
  Fill my mind with pictures of your prairies, your swamps, your
    sedge fields, your mountains and your endless plains.

Tell me too, about the times you didn't shoot for some sweet secret
    reason of your own.

I want to hear the stories about Charley and Jimmy and Ed.
  Could they build a fire?
  Did they get lost?
  Could they track?

Make me laugh with the stories about the day Irv never got a shot
    and old Belle brought him a quail, still warm, she'd found and
    put it in his hand.
  Let me hold the puppy on my lap.
  Let me scratch the old dog's belly while she warms her backside
    by the fire.
  Fill my glass again and pass me the wooden bowl with the apples
    in it.

Talk to me about the bee tree cutting.
  Tell me how deep the ice pond was.
  Show me how you call ducks.
  Tell me how you make a rabbit stew.

Who was the best shot you ever saw?
  Who always got his buck?

What's your favorite excuse of all the ones you've heard?
 Why is it, do you suppose, that men have stopped telling lies the
  way they used to do.

Take me with you to the places with the names I like.
 Take me to the Superstition Mountains where the white wing
  and mourning doves come in flights like feathered clouds.

Take me along the gentle curvings of the Tombigbee.
 Show me big horn sheep that feed above the Phophet River.
 And the elk along the Yellowstone.
 And the Badlands bear picking berries.
 And the woodcock flighting to the Merrimack.
 And the wild turkey in the Dismal Swamp.

Time does not exist where these things never change.
 Listen . . . don't you hear the same quail call and mallard
  stutters as the men in the faded brown pictures?

Sing me the old songs.

Tell me the stories of times gone by.

HUNTER'S MOON

AN ENGLISH astronomer once commented to the effect that the slight changing of the redness of a distant star could alter a hundred years of our mathematical calculations. This was his way of saying that the works of man are insignificant when faced with the whims of nature. Civilizations have been born or lost in earthquakes and the coming and going of volcanos and tidal waves. A degree or two of temperature change over a few thousand years melted away the ice cap that covered much of North America and a slight shifting in the rain patterns of the world has created bare and torrid deserts where years ago lay tropic jungle. Hairy mammoths that were born and raised in long-lost humid swamps are now chipped out of the light blue ice of our polar lands.

And you and I stand now in the coming of the fall speculating on the possibilities of an early frost that hopefully will skim the leaves from tenacious oaks . . . and yet not be severe enough to chill the ground so as to send the woodcock flying on to warmer soils and softer breezes. The slim balance of our sport so hangs on the vagaries of the unseen winds, the unknown seas—mysteries in their causes no less to us than to our apelike ancestors.

Yet, we will grow restive in the weeks ahead. The Hunter's Moon will see the shadow of a sleepless man who paces up and down his plot of grass, a morsel of dog as curious and as expectant as he is, tagging at his heels. He will stare at scudding clouds . . . wet his fingers to predict the vagrant wind . . . and hope that tomorrow will be kind enough to offer him a touch of frost or a heavy rain or a tracking snow. (And don't forget the days you have all three between the dawn and dark!)

But we'll go on out, if I know you, regardless. And come home wet or cold or both ten times to the single day we come home smiling at the red god's toss of dice. But that's all part of sport . . . small creatures are the birds and sheep and deer to us . . . and we, small creatures too, our wishes merely hopes sent up at night, cast out on the winds, in the light of the Hunter's Moon.

SEPTEMBER

SEPTEMBER IS a long walk through high and dying grass. The brook that lazes its way through my meadow has a parched, dry face. A scar of summer. My back is turned away from the months of sun and I lean forward seeking the first turn in the flavor of the wind for the coming of fall. We get absolutely hungry for the taste of change. The tinting of the trees comes first in the lowland bottoms. The swamp maples and alders are our barometer. When they are orange and yellow to the eye, then the ear begins to sharpen for the first flights of Canadas and blacks.

At the beginning the mood is one of ever-increasing quietness, a muting of the evening frogs. The hum of bees and the swarms of fire-flies change places with the doleful wailing of the mourning doves. The cock pheasants in the corn fields brag a little less loudly now and the coveys of quail begin to whisper rather than shout back and forth. The muskrats add an hour or two to their busy schedule. And even I, moved by some ancient warning, rouse myself from the hammock in the late afternoon heat and begin to think about splitting a little kindling from the chestnut logs behind the barn. But the lure of summer isn't over—quite. Good intentioned, I sharpen the hatchet and with the Labradors underfoot we start to wander through the apple trees and there fall victim to the fruit like some modern Adam. Somehow a Northern Spy or two is still gleaming russet in the higher branches waiting for a stick to set it free. The Labradors fetch the stick back for me to knock an apple down for them and then we sit, we three, and eat our just desserts while the womenfolk are hard at work back home.

September is the month God made for the lazy man. It's the month to look back on a summer's worth of work and to look forward to a shoot or so this fall. Someday soon, now, we'd best get busy and grease the boots, sort out the shells we have left over in three or four of our favorite coats and slim the hips down on our favorite dogs. But not right now. Tomorrow will be just the day to get things right. That's the sweetness of September. It's a month of tomorrows. Right now, let's go get just one more apple for the hammock and let the dogs rest in its little patch of shade while we sit and dream of more ambitious weather and the whiskbroom winds that sit in wait just around the corner to shoo the woodcock and the ducks from their northern nests and chase us from the back yard to the blinds.

A CHRISTMAS WISH

THERE ARE a lot of legends and stories about Christmas wishes
. . . and how I wish this year that wishes were real and I had one
now and then. My old dog Tip, I know, wishes she could run the
fields again instead of having to shuffle slowly at my heels. And I'd
like to wipe away the touch of winter that has come to stay forever
with some of my old shooting friends. Some folks say to be careful
of what I wish for because it might come true. But I don't think
you and I would abuse the privilege. I don't know what I'd do if I
was rich, so I wouldn't wish for that this Christmas. I'd like to take
the friendships that I deeply treasure and really stretch them out
for times to come. Old dogs, old friends, old brooks and quail
meadows that I have learned to love especially should never change
or go away. I think I know the wish that we'd all like to have. A
handful of friends . . . a handful of dogs . . . would have their
sweetest yesterdays become tomorrows.

FLINCHING

I'M ALWAYS intrigued with stories about how to break more targets and I ran across an article in *Trap & Field* that will have to be the absolute topper: "Clarence Douglass, Jr. can claim breaking 27,000 targets in one day. The targets were loaded on a truck which Douglass was driving. The truck went out of control, rolled over twice, and 27,000 targets were smashed. Douglass said he would have broken more, but he started to flinch the second time the truck flopped over."

Since I'm a grade A victim myself, I've made a sort of hobby out of collecting flinches. Basic flinching, as you probably know, is the inability to pull the trigger of a shotgun when you want to. And this can take some very interesting forms. One man, rather portly, used to carry his 25 shells for a round of trap in a small leather box on a belt around his waist. He flinched so badly after about ten shots that his belly started to buck and would throw five shells in the air out of the box at the same time. Another has a magnificent flinch. When he can't pull the trigger he starts walking toward the trap house—I've seen him cover 15 yards before he got control of himself. But we all suspect that he will eventually make it all the way to the house itself and some feel he'll even get one or two steps up on the roof.

I don't know what causes flinching and I sure as shooting

never heard of any cure. Mechanically, there is a device known as a release trigger. Needless to say I've used one for trap shooting for years. (I'll take *any* help I can get.) It's a trigger in reverse. You cock the trigger by pulling it back and it fires when you take your finger off—or release—the trigger. It's damned tricky at first, but no problem when you get used to it. There's quite some controversy about release triggers but as someone said "I never saw anybody shoot worse with one after he got it than he did before."

A few shooters who don't flinch use these triggers. They believe that the releasing motion is smoother and easier and therefore faster than pulling a trigger. On two-barreled guns you can get a release/pull set-up or go all the way with a release/release. A lot of shooters don't like to admit to using one, but a good percent more freely admit that they just couldn't shoot any kind of a decent score without one and it's simply a question of using the release or stop competitive shooting.

If a release works for flinching I imagine it would work with fumbling. What about the market for a release wallet for all those guys we know who haven't grabbed a bar check in years?

DAYDREAMS

ONE OF the problems of writing is that the editors insist, secure in the knowledge that all writers are lazy dogs, that the work be turned in months in advance. Consequently when you're writing, for example, a piece due for May, your body is sitting in frigid February while your mind is somewhere in the warmer future— shooting trap in shirtsleeves. The whole problem is anticipation. But when you stop to mull that over you find, more often than not, that anticipation is a helluva lot of what everything is all about.

You'll have to grant that anticipation sees more quail on the table than reality by roughly two to one . . . depending on how much of a dreamer you are.

Now anticipation is different than plain wishful thinking. Anticipation must have some grounds in fact. For example: I wish I'll find some nice old lady who has this old shotgun for sale. And this old shotgun will turn out to be a CHE Grade Parker, 20-gauge, with a single trigger and a straight hand stock. And she'll let it go for $20; throwing in a brass bound trunk case made of half-inch thick English hide. That's pure wishing at its worst. But to *anticipate* this happening you'd only have to change the facts a bit—like the sweet little old lady will turn out to be Abercrombie & Fitch and the $20 will average out near $400 and change.

But there are things we can anticipate without really nudging the laws of probability too hard. I have a short list of things that I've made my family commit to memory—in anticipation of their turning up someday: A Ward Brother's pintail decoy for $20.00. A nice color print of A. B. Frost's "Woodcock Shooting"—either spring or fall, since there are two, for under $30. A darned good copy of *New England Grouse Shooting* by Foster—for its original price of around $10.

So far not much luck . . . but knowing what these things were worth not too far back in time . . . I can anticipate.

Then there are the more advanced states of anticipation . . . like having your best buddy drive eight hours to meet you for a shoot and find the black ducks thick as flies and he remembered you like Virginia Gentleman bourbon and laid some in for after dark. Or having a favorite pipe you've lost for so long you can't really remember turn up in an old shooting coat you forgot you even had until your wife began cleaning the attic.

Or having a close neighbor tell you he's got one of the best woodcock and quail pointers in the state and discovering that by God, he really does!

Needless to say we're talking about the once in a coon's age, but a dyed-in-the-wool anticipator has a right to anticipate optimistically!

THE FUNERAL

It was the kind of day you'd expect for a funeral. The northeast wind was grizzled with rain and heavy grey clouds lumbered about the sky so dismally that the mere memory of sunshine seemed absurd. But all the animals that could get there were there. They clustered into small groups more or less according to age, like humans do, while waiting for the hearse. Some wandered reflectively around the graveyard staring at the various headstones and the stone vaults. They stood before the marker of the passenger pigeon a minute or two and then passed by the crypt of the woods bison, where some of the larger ones, like the timber wolf and the grizzly, lingered. A few of the birds who had come a long way— the whooping crane from Texas and the condor and brown pelican from California—chatted softly near a tilted headstone that marked the heath hen.

Some of the bolder ones stole glances at the pelican and the condor, both of whom bore the telltale look. Their feathers were dull and wispy and they hung their heads a bit more than you'd expect from just the fatigue of such a long journey. The pelican still had traces of crude oil along the bottom of his pouched beak; now and then he absent-mindedly wiped at it with his wing but merely succeeded in smearing it around. One of the alligators that had come from the Everglades stared at them so intently it verged on rudeness, but curiously no one seemed to care.

Some of the smaller birds, like the woodcock and the kingfisher, started the old rumor again about a cure for DDT, but few paid any attention except for the loons and the mergansers, which were largely just looking for someone to talk to anyway.

As usual much of the conversation centered about those that couldn't come. The clams, the Atlantic salmon, the shad which, up until recently, had attended all the funerals.

The bald eagle began to complain about the upper air, coughing every so often, to punctuate his remarks. And inevitably the conversation turned to the Great Lakes, the Hudson River, the Delaware, California beaches, several of the great southern swamps and the Canadian prairies. The ducks, which traveled a great deal and usually tried to dominate the talk, did no more than nod in agreement until the end when a hen redhead told about the experience her neighbors were having with lead poisoning, and her own problems about not being able to find a place to raise her family over the last summer.

But few were really paying close attention. They had heard it all before and stood around staring into the distance and now and then cocking an ear or turning toward the road where they expected any minute to see the hearse.

As they waited the wind began to freshen and the familiar acrid odor of sulphur drifted over them from a distant pulpmill. In the same tones that they had used in dredging their memories about the days of fresh water and succulent grasses the talk wove around the old homes they had known. Redwoods, the towering fork of the American elm and the soft cool shade of the sheltering chestnut in summers too long past. Some even remembered the singular mast-filled forests of the huge white pines. Others recalled the black cypress, and the waterbirds murmured about the ebb and flow of the tidal eelgrass. Near the grave of the masked quail, a pair of prairie chickens reminisced about the old farm hedgerows and the harvests before the time of the machines.

The grizzly, impatient with all this doleful chatter, began to aimlessly rake through some heavy tufts of grass in hopes of finding a mouse for a tidbit, but stopped when he heard an owl clattering his beak at him for being so silly as to have forgotten what happened to mice—and if some had escaped so far—it was a foolhardy thing to eat one.

His indigestion had come back and the grizzly was about to ask around about any new berries that someone might have found when the sound of a motor was heard.

They lined up along both edges of the road so that the hearse passed between them and then turned and followed it to the place where a mound of bare earth lay beside a small grave.

The same words that had been used so many times before were spoken once again. "Progress . . . in the name of civilization . . . scientific triumph for the larger good . . . etc. etc. etc."

The box was lowered. The clods of dirt slapped hollowly against each other until only a scar of water remained in the sere grass, muddily reflecting the one word OSPREY and the date.

Some of the birds flew off together. The wolf and the grizzly separated and left alone. The alligator stayed, blinking his eyes, until almost everyone had left, then he, too, with one last look at the resting place of an old friend, stumped off. The eagle, the pelican and the condor, however, didn't move. Nor did they speak. It was as if their homeward journey was too far . . . and too futile for such an effort. They would stay here. It would be just a matter of time.